T0323832

"In 1978 J. I. Packer delivered these lectures at Reformed Bible College in Michigan then traveled to Australia to present the second series of Annual Moore College Lectures. So we have been waiting forty-five years for them to be published! However, precisely because of the long gap between delivery and publication, this book is able to challenge us powerfully about how far we have fallen from those days. These chapters remind us of vintage Packer: the calm and courteous style, the unrelenting focus on the Lord Jesus our Savior and faithfulness to the Scriptures, and an incisive perspective on the movements shaping the world in which we live as Christian disciples. This book is certainly worth reading, and I highly commend it."

Mark D. Thompson, Principal, Moore Theological College

"J. I. Packer set a high standard for proclaiming the gospel of Christ. His arguments were gracious but never cowardly, strong but never strident, faithful but never repetitive. Now with the publication of his 1978 lectures, we are all enriched more deeply for 'the defense and confirmation of the gospel' (Phil. 1:7) in our generation."

Ray Ortlund, President, Renewal Ministries

"In my youth, I was bombarded with teaching that denied the absolute uniqueness of Christ. We were told that such an assertion was based on a few proof texts which ran counter to the overall message of the Bible. At that time the writings and tape-recorded messages of J. I. Packer helped convince me that our affirmation of uniqueness was based primarily not only on a few proof texts, but upon the person and work of Christ who was the Creator's answer to the dilemma faced by his creation. I'm so happy to see this material in circulation in a new format. The issue is even more critical today than it was in my youth. This robust exposition by Packer is both timely and powerfully convincing."

Ajith Fernando, Teaching Director, Youth for Christ, Sri Lanka; author, *Discipling in a Multicultural World*

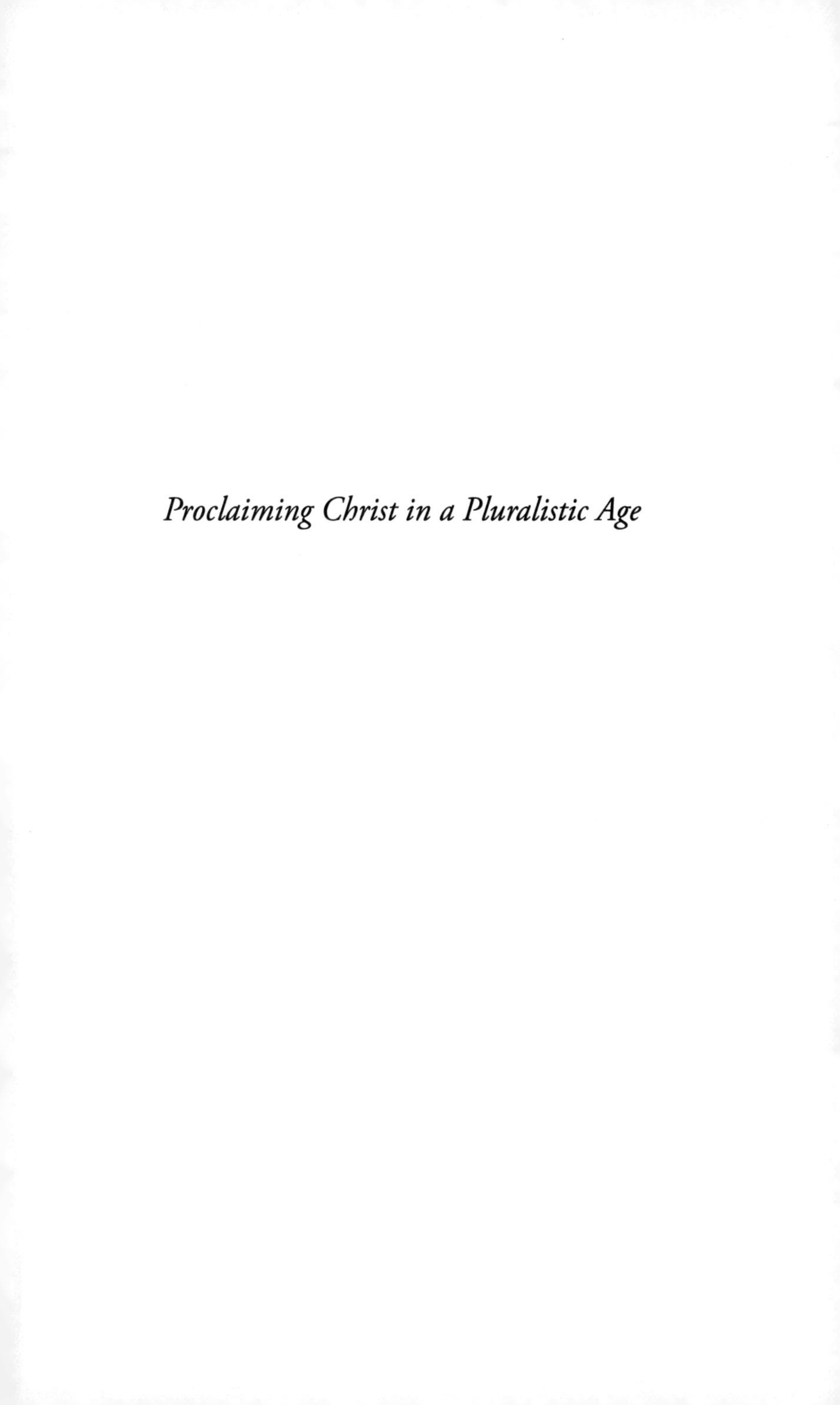

Proclaiming Christ in a Pluralistic Age

Proclaiming Christ in a Pluralistic Age

The 1978 Lectures

J. I. Packer

WHEATON, ILLINOIS

Proclaiming Christ in a Pluralistic Age: The 1978 Lectures

Published by Crossway
1300 Crescent Street
Wheaton, Illinois 60187

Cover design: Jordan Singer

Cover image: Dr. J. I. Packer, "He Emptied Himself: The Divinity of Jesus Christ," Lecture 3, Annual Moore College Lectures, Sydney, Australia, September 1978.

First printing 2024

Printed in the United States of America

All emphases in Scripture quotations have been added by the author.

Hardcover ISBN: 978-1-4335-8530-2
ePub ISBN: 978-1-4335-8533-3
PDF ISBN: 978-1-4335-8531-9

Library of Congress Cataloging-in-Publication Data

Names: Packer, J. I. (James Innell), author.
Title: Proclaiming Christ in a pluralistic age : the 1978 lectures / J.I.Packer.
Description: Wheaton, Illinois : Crossway, 2024. | Includes index.
Identifiers: LCCN 2023005878 (print) | LCCN 2023005879 (ebook) | ISBN 9781433585302 (hardcover) | ISBN 9781433585319 (pdf) | ISBN 9781433585333 (epub)
Subjects: LCSH: Bible.—Luke—Criticism, interpretation. | Crucifixion—Religious aspect—Christianity.
Classification: LCC BS2595.52 .P34 2024 (print) | LCC BS2595.52 (ebook) | DDC 226.4/06—dc23/eng/20231003
LC record available at https://lccn.loc.gov/2023005878
LC ebook record available at https://lccn.loc.gov/2023005879

Crossway is a publishing ministry of Good News Publishers.

LB 33 32 31 30 29 28 27 26 25 24
15 14 13 12 11 10 9 8 7 6 5 4 3 2 1

The 1978 Reformed Bible College Baker Mission Lectures
Grand Rapids, Michigan
The 1978 Moore Theological College Lectures
Sydney, Australia

Contents

Outline

5. No Other Name: The Uniqueness of Jesus Christ

- Theological Truth
  - The Purpose of the Cross
  - The Person of the Cross
  - The Event of the Cross
  - The Truth of the Cross
  - The Witnesses of the Cross
  - The Preaching of the Cross
  - The Claim of the Cross
  - The Need for the Cross
- Theological Speculations
  - Pluralism: All Religions Save
  - Roman Catholicism: Anonymous Christians Will Be Saved
  - Universalism: All Will Be Saved
    1. Universalism and Man's Decisions
    2. Universalism and Gospel Preaching
    3. Universalism and Christian Conscience
- A Perishing World
- A Sovereign God
- An Urgent Call

Publisher's Preface

The Life and Legacy of J. I. Packer

J. I. Packer (1926–2020) was a lifelong Anglican churchman who spent the first half of his life in England and the second half in Canada but who was perhaps most popular in the United States. He is widely recognized as one of the most influential theological popularizers of the twentieth century.[1]

James Innell Packer was born on July 22, 1926, in the village of Twyning in the north of Gloucestershire, England, the firstborn child of James and Dorothy Packer. His only sibling, Margaret, was born in 1929. The Packers were a lower–middle-class family with a nominal Anglican faith, faithfully attending

1 Portions of this preface are adapted from Justin Taylor, "J. I. Packer (1926–2020)," TGC, July 17, 2020, https://www.thegospelcoalition.org. For biographies and studies of Packer, see in particular, Alister McGrath, *J. I. Packer: His Life and Thought* (Downers Grove, IL: InterVarsity, 2020); Leland Ryken, *J. I. Packer: An Evangelical Life* (Wheaton, IL: Crossway, 2015); Sam Storms, *Packer on the Christian Life: Knowing God in Christ, Walking by the Spirit* (Wheaton, IL: Crossway, 2015); Timothy George, ed., *J. I. Packer and the Evangelical Future: The Impact of His Life and Thought* (Grand Rapids, MI: Baker Academic, 2009); Don J. Payne, *The Theology of the Christian Life in J. I. Packer's Thought* (Eugene, OR: Wipf and Stock, 2006).

nearby St. Catharine's Church but never talking about the things of God or even praying before meals.

In September of 1933, at the age of seven, young Packer was chased by a bully at junior school out into the street and violently collided with a passing bread van. The traumatic injury resulted in brain surgery, a three-week hospital stay, and six months of recuperation at home away from school. He had a depressed compound fracture of the frontal bone on the right-hand side of his forehead—he later compared it to the way the top of an eggshell is knocked in when hit with an egg spoon. A skilled surgeon at his local hospital was able to extract the bits of broken bone. The doctor required him to wear a black, protective aluminum plate over his injury, held in place by an elastic band. He was forbidden from playing any sports, causing the young man, already prone to being a loner, to confine himself even further to activities like reading and writing. He wore the protective plate for the next eight years, and then at the age of fifteen, refused to wear it again.

On the morning of his eleventh birthday, in 1937, Packer awoke hoping to find a bicycle waiting for him—a traditional coming-of-age gift for English boys. He had dropped hints. Instead, his parents gave him a used, heavy Oliver typewriter in excellent condition. His biographer Alister McGrath notes the spiritual lesson: "It was not what Packer had asked for; nevertheless, it proved to be what he needed. . . . his best present and the most treasured possession of his boyhood."[2]

That fall, in 1937, Packer transitioned from junior school to the Crypt School, which counted among its former students

2 McGrath, *J. I. Packer*, 6.

the eighteenth-century preacher and evangelist George Whitefield. Packer became the only student in his class to specialize in "classics."

Packer was confirmed at their family church, St. Catherine's, at the age of fourteen having never heard about conversion or saving faith.

At the age of eighteen, Packer won a scholarship to Oxford University, studying classics at Corpus Christi College. He arrived in Oxford as an awkward, shy, intellectual oddball (his own description), with a single suitcase in hand. His father, a clerk for the Great Western Railway, was able to secure for his son a free ticket for the hour-long train ride.

Three weeks later, on October 22, 1944, Packer attended a Sunday evening evangelistic sermon at St. Aldate's Church. An elderly Anglican parson gave the address. The biblical exposition left Packer bored, but in the second half, the pastor recounted how at a boys' camp he had been challenged as to whether he was really a Christian. Packer recognized himself in the story and realized he did not know Christ. Following the invitation, which concluded with the singing of "Just as I Am" (written by Charlotte Elliot in 1835), Packer trusted in Jesus Christ as Savior for his sins and as Lord of his life. He was just yards away from where Whitefield had converted in 1735.

That same year, in 1944, a retired Anglican clergyman, losing his eyesight, donated his large library to the Oxford Inter-Collegiate Christian Union. The leaders of OICCU stored them in a basement and asked Packer the bookworm if he wanted to sort through the sets, including classics from the sixteenth and seventeenth centuries.

Packer soon came across an uncut set of the writings of the seventeenth-century Puritan, John Owen. Packer noted with interest the volume on temptation and sin. He cut the volume open and devoured the contents. Years later he wrote: "I owe more, I think, to John Owen than to any other theologian, ancient or modern, and I am sure I owe more to his little book on mortification than to anything else he wrote."[3] Packer would go on to adopt the Puritan model of the pious pastor-scholar. In fact, he asked people to think of him as a latter-day Puritan: "One who, like those great seventeenth-century leaders on both sides of the Atlantic, seeks to combine in himself the roles of scholar, preacher, and pastor, and speaks to you out of that purpose."[4]

After obtaining his BA degree from Corpus Christi in Oxford (1948), he took up his first teaching post at Oak Hill Theological College in London as a tutor (instructor) in Greek and Latin (along with some philosophy). For the next three years, Packer studied for ordination at Wycliffe Hall, Oxford, and then did doctoral research. He was ordained as a deacon in the Church of England in 1952, then as a priest at Birmingham Cathedral in 1953. From 1952 to 1954, he served as a curate (associate pastor) at St. John's in Harborne, a suburb of Birmingham, while finishing his four-hundred-page doctoral dissertation on the Puritan Richard Baxter at Oxford University. He was awarded the MA and DPhil degrees in 1954.

3 J. I. Packer, "Introduction," *Puritan Portraits* (Fearn, Ross-shire, UK: Christian Focus, 2012), 1.

4 J. I. Packer, "Inerrancy and the Divinity and Humanity of the Bible," in *Honouring the Written Word of God: The Collected Shorter Writings of J. I. Packer*, vol. 3 (Vancouver: Regent College Publishing, 2008), 162.

On July 17, 1954, Packer married Kit Mullett, a Welsh nurse whom he had met after a speaking engagement in Surrey in the late spring of 1952. Together they would go on to adopt three children: Ruth, Naomi, and Martin.

The Packers moved to Bristol in 1955, where Packer served as a lecturer at Tyndale Hall. In 1961, the Packers moved back to Oxford, where for the next nine years he served as librarian and then warden at Latimer House—an evangelical research center begun by Packer and John Stott to theologically strengthen the Church of England.

In 1970, Packer returned to Tyndale Hall as principal. The following year, Tyndale Hall was incorporated into the new Trinity College, Bristol, where Alec Motyer was named principal and Packer the associate principal. The move freed Packer to have more time to write.

In the early 1970s, Packer approached Inter-Varsity Press about publishing a series of articles he had written in the 1960s for *Evangelical Magazine*. The publisher responded that they needed him to write on the charismatic issue sweeping through Great Britain before they would consider a book from him on another subject. As a result, he took it to Hodder & Stoughton instead, who gladly accepted it for publication. InterVarsity Press in the United States agreed to pick up the North American rights. The book was published in 1973 with the title *Knowing God*. This work, more than any other, established his international fame and went on to sell over a million and a half copies. "The conviction behind the book," he wrote, "is that ignorance of God . . . lies at the root of much of the church's weakness today."[5]

5 J. I. Packer, *Knowing God* (Wheaton, IL: Crossway, 2023), *xiv*.

In February of 1977, Packer met with R. C. Sproul, John Gerstner, Norman Geisler, and Greg Bahnsen for a conference on the authority of Scripture at Mount Hermon, California. Later that year, the International Council on Biblical Inerrancy was formed, which produced the Chicago Statement on Biblical Inerrancy in 1978, with Sproul as the lead author.

In 1979, James Houston, who had been friends with Packer since their undergraduate days at Oxford, invited him to join the faculty at Regent College at Vancouver. Packer eventually accepted the position, which would allow him to teach without administrative duties, and his family made the transatlantic relocation. He maintained a position at the university until the end of his life, retiring from full-time teaching in 1996 and teaching part time thereafter.

In the late 1990s, Packer accepted an invitation from Lane Dennis, president and CEO of Crossway, to serve as the general editor of the English Standard Version, a revision of the Revised Standard Version, which itself was in the historic English-language lineage of the King James Bible. The ESV was published in 2001. Packer reflected in the winter years of his life on his involvement with this Bible translation: "I find myself suspecting very strongly that this was the most important thing that I have ever done for the Kingdom."[6]

Packer's "last crusade" was devoted to helping the church recover catechesis (instruction in the Christian faith). This work culminated in *To Be a Christian: An Anglican Catechism*—the catechism of the Anglican Church in North America (ACNA).

6 J. I. Packer, comments at a banquet hosted by Crossway at the International Christian Retail Show, 2006.

Packer sometimes wondered if commentators on his theological and ministerial career had missed his personal side, including the humor that he saw in life and the twinkle in his eye. He did not want to be portrayed as a brain in a vat or a mere purveyor of theological ideas. His longtime friend Timothy George described what it was like to watch the man in action:

> His smile is irrepressible and his laughter can bring light to the most somber of meetings. His love for all things human and humane shines through. His mastery of ideas and the most fitting words in which to express them is peerless. Ever impatient with shams of all kinds, his saintly character and spirituality run deep.[7]

In 2015, while filming a short documentary on Packer for Crossway, it came time for a final question. He was asked how he might want to be remembered someday when he was gone. He paused, in his characteristic way before answering any question (no matter how routine), took a breath, and responded:

> As I look back on the life that I have lived, I would like to be remembered as a voice—a voice that focused on the authority of the Bible, the glory of our Lord Jesus Christ, the wonder of his substitutionary sacrifice and atonement for our sins.
>
> I would like to be remembered as a voice calling Christian people to holiness and challenging lapses in Christian moral standards.

7 Timothy George, "Introduction," *J. I. Packer and the Evangelical Future: The Impact of His Life and Thought*, ed. Timothy George (Grand Rapids, MI: Baker Academic, 2009), 11.

> I should like to be remembered as someone who was always courteous in controversy but without compromise.
>
> I ask you to thank God with me for the way that he has led me, and I wish, hope, pray that you will enjoy the same clear leading from him and the same help in doing the tasks that he sets you that I have enjoyed. And if your joy matches my joy as we continue in our Christian lives, well, you will be blessed indeed.[8]

J. I. Packer went to be with the Lord on July 17, 2020, at his home in Vancouver at the age of ninety-three.

This Posthumous Book

In 2020, Pastor Griffin Gulledge of Madison Baptist Church in Georgia, himself a PhD candidate in systematic theology at Southeastern Baptist Theological Seminary, posted on his blog five black-and-white videos of Packer lecturing at Moore Theological College in Sydney, Australia, from 1978.[9] Crossway had the lectures transcribed and initially edited by freelance editor Karalee Reinke.

Further research on the provenance of this material reveals that Packer delivered these lectures first at Reformed Bible College (now Kuyper College) in Grand Rapids, Michigan, and they were lightly revised for presentation at Moore. Though the intention was that the lectures would be published as a book, this never materialized.

8 "J. I. Packer: In His Own Words," Crossway Articles, July 18, 2020, https://www.crossway.org.

9 Griffin Gulledge, "J. I. Packer's 1978 Moore College Lectures," Contra Mundum, https://griffingulledge.com.

In the course of these lectures, there are some sections of the lectures (as documented at relevant sections in the notes in this book) that were repurposed from previously published articles, in particular one of the lectures that Packer delivered at Dallas Theological Seminary in April of 1972 as part of the W. H. Griffith Thomas Memorial Lectures and a lecture delivered in July of 1973 at Tyndale House, Cambridge, on the logic of penal substitution. We are grateful to all of these institutions for their cordial cooperation.

The lectures in this book constitute a narrative that begins in eternity past, culminates in the cross of Calvary, where both the person and work of Christ are expounded, and then applies the good news to our own day.

Packer begins by noting that the Jews required signs and the Greeks sought wisdom—and today intellectuals seek wisdom and liberals seek needs—but we have a different and better story to tell, the story of Christ crucified and risen. This many-stranded story—of God's kingdom, people, mediation, victory, Son, and image—is the true story that must be proclaimed today for all to hear.

In the second lecture, Packer looks at the humanity of Jesus the Messiah, the Son of God, the only way to the Father and thus our only hope. Packer describes and refutes the modern humanitarian views swirling in the 1970s.

Packer's third lecture turns from Christ's humanity to focus on his divinity as eternal God, suffering servant, and incarnate Son. He considers the kenosis theory of Christ emptying himself of his attributes and finds it wanting before proposing his own understanding that seeks to take into account all of the biblical witness.

The fourth lecture moves from the person of Christ to the work of Christ, glorying in the wonderful exchange. Packer works through various categories of the cross—sacrifice, ransom, redemption, and propitiation—before expounding in greater depth the categories of substitution and satisfaction.

Finally, in the last lecture, Packer looks at the uniqueness of Christ. As with all of the other lectures, he first sets forth theological truth—looking at the cross from the angles of the purpose, person, event, truth, witness, preaching, claim, and need. He then sets his sights on three challenges to the uniqueness of Christ: pluralism (all religions save); Roman Catholicism (anonymous Christians will be saved); and universalism (all will be saved).

The lectures are vintage Packer. With the apostle Paul, he gloried in the cross, boasting in it alone, and was convinced that its proclamation was essential in every age, especially our pluralistic one. Though these lectures bear the marks of their age, delivered forty-five years ago, the message is eternally relevant. We have sought to edit them with a light hand, adding subheadings and citations, as well as smoothing out the prose as required for its written form. We have resisted editing it so heavily that it loses some of its original flavor as oral addresses.

Throughout his nearly seventy years of public ministry, in the classroom, at churches, and through his writings, Packer stressed the importance of knowing and praying to and communing with the triune God. He called for the church to take holiness and repentance seriously by walking in the Spirit and fighting against indwelling sin. He defended biblical authority and championed the cause of disciple-making catechesis. And he reintroduced multiple generations to his beloved Puritan forebears, whom he regarded as the Redwoods of the Christian faith.

He saw himself as "a voice that called people back to old paths of truth and wisdom." His entire life was spent resisting the idea that "the newer is the truer, only what is recent is decent, every shift of ground is a step forward, and every latest word must be hailed as the last word on its subject."[10] Though he was willing to address and engage the controversies of his day, he wrote, "I should like to be remembered as one who pointed to the pasturelands."

May the lectures captured in this book point you to the pasturelands as you walk with the Good Shepherd who is the Savior of the world.

10 J. I. Packer, "Is Systematic Theology a Mirage? An Introductory Discussion," in *Doing Theology in Today's World: Essays in Honor of Kenneth S. Kantzer*, ed. John D. Woodbridge and Thomas Edward McComiskey (Grand Rapids, MI: Zondervan, 1991), 21.

1

We've a Story to Tell

We Preach Christ Crucified

The Antithesis of the Gospel

The apostle Paul set forth his gospel to the Corinthians:

> We preach Christ crucified, a stumbling block [*skandalon*] to Jews and folly [*mória*] to Gentiles, but to those who are called, both Jews and Greeks, Christ the power of God and the wisdom of God. (1 Cor. 1:23–24)

In so doing, Paul put his gospel in antithesis to two first-century forms of intellectual self-assertion:

> Jews demand signs and Greeks seek wisdom. (1 Cor. 1:22)

Two attitudes reveal this self-assertion: by the *questions* that they asked about the gospel and by their *reactions* to the gospel. By these, the questions and the reactions, you shall know them.

The Unreasonable Skepticism of Jews Requiring Signs

There was the attitude first of the Jews. The Jews required a sign, says Paul. What does that mean? That the Jews were hard-headed realists, unwilling to advance a step beyond evidence? No, it means nothing of the kind. It means that the Jews were showing themselves unreasonable skeptics. The sign, which the Jews required in those days, was a type of evidence that we may describe as miracles and magic to order.

The second temptation which had been put to our Lord Jesus Christ in the wilderness had taken the form of an invitation to provide miracles and magic to order. Remember how the devil tempted the Lord basically saying, "Throw yourself down from a pinnacle of the temple and get up unhurt at the bottom, and you'll wow them" (cf. Matt. 4:5–6)? That was the essence of the temptation. And Jesus had refused it. He was not gathering support, not gathering followers, on that basis. And so we read that when "the Pharisees came and began to argue with him, seeking from him a sign from heaven to test him, he sighed deeply in his spirit and said, 'Why does this generation seek a sign? Truly I say to you, no sign will be given to this generation.' And he left them" (Mark 8:11–13).

These requests are really skepticism masquerading as interest. At bottom, it's an attitude of unwillingness to believe. What is being demanded? Miracles and magic to order is something that it is arrogant and arbitrary to demand in a situation where abundant signs had already been given. That's what we have to grasp. In the ministry of our Lord Jesus Christ—as those who watched it saw it and as it was reported by the apostle Paul to the Corinthians and others—abundant signs had been given already.

Do you remember how, in the opening verses of Matthew 11, we are told of the messengers who came from John the Baptist, languishing in prison, to ask the Lord Jesus, "Are you the one who is to come, or shall we look for another?" (Matt. 11:3)? And this was John's question.

Some of the things that Jesus had been doing, and even more perhaps things that Jesus had *not* been doing, had surprised John. John's idea, based on the way that God had prompted him to herald the coming Messiah, was that as soon as Jesus's ministry began, catastrophic things would begin to happen: acts of judgment, acts of traumatic import for the life of the nation.

Jesus had not been ministering in that way. Hence the question, Are you he who should come? The one "whose fan is in his hand" to "purge his floor" (Matt. 3:12 KJV), or are we to look for someone else?

And do you remember how Jesus replied to John's question? The message that he sent back through John's disciples was this: "Go and tell John what you hear and see—the blind receive their sight and the lame walk, lepers are cleansed and the deaf hear, and the dead are raised up, and the poor have good news preached to them" (Matt. 11:4–5). Go and tell John that those things are happening and say to him, "Blessed is the one who is not *offended* by me," or caused to stumble (11:6). It's a word from this same root from which *skandalon* comes. Blessed is he who should not be caused to stumble at me. Blessed is he who discerns the meaning of the signs that are being given in my ministry and is prepared to trust me concerning those matters where I happen to fulfill these expectations.

But the signs that had been given were the decisive ones. For what Jesus meant for John to pick up was this: that here was being fulfilled what Isaiah long ago had prophesied. We know the words well. They're in the thirty-fifth chapter of the prophecy, and Handel set them to memorable music in the *Messiah.* "Then the eyes of the blind shall be opened," Isaiah had predicted, "and the ears of the deaf shall be unstopped. Then shall the lame man leap as an hart, and the tongue of the dumb sing" (Isa. 35:5–6 KJV). That's how it shall be in the day when God visits his people to bless them.

Yes, the signs had been given. And a further sign was to be given. Jesus refers to that in the opening verses of Matthew 16, where again we find him asked for a sign. "The Pharisees and Sadducees came, and to test him they asked him to show them a sign from heaven. He answered them, . . . 'An evil and adulterous generation seeks for a sign, but no sign will be given to it except the sign of Jonah'" (Matt. 16:1–2, 4). And elsewhere he'd interpreted that reference "as Jonah was three days and three nights in the belly of the great fish, so will the Son of Man be three days and three nights in the heart of the earth" (Matt. 12:40). And after that, not. After that, alive again.

The sign of resurrection was to be given to confirm the witness born by those miraculous healings and works of mercy that Jesus did during his three-year ministry in Galilee. The signs *had* been given. That's the point to grasp.

But the Jews who heard the stories still sought a sign. They wouldn't accept the signs that had been given, because they'd not been given to order. The Jews, you might say, demanded to call the shots, to specify what signs should be given and where. They wanted to make God, as it were, dance to their tune. This is frivolous skepticism. It's an expression of dispositional unbelief. *Can't* believe, in this situation, means *won't* believe.

The Jews unreasonably required signs. Many signs had been given, which already they were ignoring. Jesus put his finger on dispositional unbelief, resolute skepticism, when at the end of his story of the rich man and Lazarus, he said this, "If they do not hear Moses and the Prophets, neither will they be convinced if someone should rise from the dead" (Luke 16:31). I don't think that needs any explanatory comment from me.

The Invasive Intellectualism of Greeks Seeking Wisdom

The Greeks, Paul continued, seek after wisdom. What does that mean? Is the quest for wisdom a sign of great and superior intelligence? Doubtless the Greeks themselves would have insisted that it was, for they regarded themselves as folk of great and superior intelligence. But we have to say no. This request for wisdom is not that. It is a mark rather of invasive intellectualism, which is something rather different.

What was the wisdom that they asked Paul to provide? What they were seeking was a type of communication to which they were accustomed and in which they were interested. And probably there are two things in mind here as Paul speaks.

Some sought philosophical speculations on the world and life and things, speculations based on flights of audacious reason. Others were doubly seeking the kind of *gnosis*, inside knowledge, that was offered by the mystery cults. That too was often called wisdom in the first century AD. What it consisted of was the provision of occult secrets giving supernatural power, putting the adherent of the mystery cult in the know regarding all kinds of what were supposed to be spiritual mysteries, making him feel therefore that he was one of the spiritual elite.

And these were the two types of wisdom that they were asking Paul to provide. What are we to say of the Jews and the Greeks? As Paul describes them, they correspond to well-known and familiar types. Here are attitudes that are very far from dead.

You have met the man who says, "I want scientific facts. I want scientific proof before I'll believe." And he reserves the right to designate what he will regard as scientific proof, and what he will not regard as scientific proof. That man is the spiritual successor of the Jews.

Similarly you have met the man who says, "I am a man of reason. I am guided by reason. I steer by truths of reason. Whatever you have to say to me, you must present to me as a truth of reason, or I shan't take it seriously and you can't expect me to." And that man is the spiritual descendant of the Greeks.

We Preach Christ Crucified

Neither the Jew-type nor the Greek-type is willing to take things from God by revelation. This was the controversy that the gospel raised and that Paul in his testimony had to pursue constantly in the world to which he went. For Paul went proclaiming what 1 Corinthians 1:18 calls the "word of the cross." "We preach Christ crucified," he said (1:23).

Now, this certainly was a startling thing for any man to say. The Christ—that's a title, an office title as Presbyterians would say—is God's anointed world ruler, the one whom Paul in the first ten verses of this chapter had referred to no less than six times as "the Lord Jesus Christ":

- *Jesus*, the personal name;
- *Christ*, the office title; and
- *Lord*, the standard title in the ancient world given to folk who ought to be worshiped.

And Christ, says Paul, we preach as crucified. That is, we proclaim that he was executed as an outlaw. Because it was only the outlaws who were crucified in the ancient world. Capital punishment was given for grave offenses and civil rebellion.

You can see how paradoxical and startling that sounds. You can see too how humbling a message it is, as Paul explains it. For if you asked Paul what it meant that Christ the anointed world ruler whom God had designated was crucified, his reply was that "Christ died for our sins in accordance with the scriptures" (1 Cor. 15:3). There was no way in which man could be brought to God, save that the Christ should die for man's sins.

Every man has sins that need to be forgiven, and no man by his own endeavors can put those sins away. But when Paul preached his message of Christ crucified, his word of life and hope for the world immediately gave offense to the Jews. First, it cheapened their own private messianic hopes. Second, it suggested that God was weak in allowing the Messiah to go to the cross. Paul speaks ironically of "the weakness of God" (1 Cor. 1:25), obviously echoing the things the Jewish critics said about his message. It does make God appear weak, and it does focus on the putting away of sin, which to the ordinary Jew (trusting as he was in the sacrifices offered in the temple) seemed simply an irrelevant message.

Similarly, when Paul preached of Christ crucified to the Greeks, it seemed nonsense, and they said so. Paul is obviously echoing ironically what the Greeks said when he speaks of "the foolishness of God" (1 Cor. 1:25). This is a very silly story, said his Greek critics. And to them too the message of the putting away of sin by the death of the Messiah seemed irrelevant to their own felt needs. So they rejected the message, and Paul says, "This is the reaction of 'those perishing'" (cf. 1:18). When he uses that word, his language is clinical rather than emotional. He's using the word because it expresses the thought that he wants to convey, that which is perishing (according to the dictionary meaning of the Greek word *epilume* that's being used here) is that which is becoming incapable of its intended function. And that is the thought here: that men who were made for fellowship with God are showing themselves incapable of it and confirming themselves in that very incapacity by their resolute rejection of the word of the cross.

But Paul contrasts the negative reaction of those who are perishing with the positive reaction of those whom he describes as "called" (1:24), "who are being saved" (1:18). To them he says, "The message is the good word of Christ, 'the power of God and the wisdom of God'" (cf. 1:24). The power of God for part of the message is the proclaiming of his resurrection and his reign, and his power in the regeneration of sinners, and his power in the world is to see it at his return. And the message of Christ crucified is a proclamation of the wisdom of God, for, as Paul goes on to say in verse 30, Christ of God is made to us believers

- *wisdom*, meaning the way to God, and
- *righteousness*, a just justification that only divine wisdom could have devised, and

- *sanctification*, which in this verse certainly means a covenant relationship or a means of covenant relationship with God. (It means that, before it means anything else.)
- And so *redemption*, for salvation from sin.

Christ is made to us all those things in the sense that we have them all in him. This is the wisdom of God *par excellence*, says Paul, for this is God in Christ providing us with all that we need for that life for which we were made and for which sin has unfitted us.

So Paul in this passage, as often elsewhere in his writings, draws out the antithesis between faith and unbelief, between the reaction to the gospel of those who are alive and to whom therefore it comes as a savor of life for life, and those who are spiritually dead, to whom therefore the gospel comes as a savor of death unto death.

The Antithesis of the Gospel Today

The point I am laboring to make sets the perspective that we shall be exploring throughout this book, namely, that *the antithesis continues*. It continues as the gospel confronts the modern world. And it continues, alas, as the gospel confronts a great deal that goes on in the modern church. For the spiritual descendants of the Jews and the Greeks of Paul's day have got into the modern church, at least in principle and in their thought-forms. The movement that used to be called *liberalism* or *modernism* and is now frequently called *radicalism* in Christian theology manifests the same pride of mind.

I stress here that I'm speaking of the intellectual method of the movement rather than the motives of any particular individuals caught up in it. I'm speaking not of individuals but of ways of thinking. The movement, I say, manifests the same pride of mind, the same arbitrary skepticism, the same invasive intellectualism as you saw in the Jews and the Greeks of Paul's day. Still we have the arbitrary skeptics who believe that they're in a position to tell us that such realities as incarnation and resurrection cannot be. And we shall be making reference as we go along to that unhappy book, *The Myth of God Incarnate*, published by a number of English university theologians in 1977, which is just one of the latest expressions of this position. But its title, as you see, tells all at this point.[1]

Intellectuals Seek Wisdom

Evasive intellectualism refuses to take seriously the fact that God has revealed himself in history and insists on turning Jesus Christ as proclaimed in the gospel into an idea, a myth, a symbol, a memory, an image, an influence, which refuses to allow that his status is that of a divine, personal Savior.

Those who do their thinking within the line set by this movement are obliged in consequence to change the Christian message so that it's no longer an invitation from a living Savior in the terms of Matthew 11:28–29: "Come to me, all who labor and are heavy laden, and I will give you rest. Take my yoke upon you, and learn from me, for I am gentle and lowly in heart, and you shall find rest for your souls." No longer can they think of becoming a Christian in the terms in which Paul spells it out in 1 Thessalonians 1:9–10, where he says that the Thessalonian converts

1 The book, edited by theologian and philosopher of religion John Hick (1922–2012) was published one year prior to Packer's lectures at Moore. All of the contributors were professors at Birmingham, Oxford, or Cambridge.

"turned to God from idols to serve the living and true God, and to wait for his Son from heaven, whom he raised from the dead, Jesus who delivers us from the wrath to come."

No, their gospel is rather a matter of, "Come unto an influence within the church," than it is a matter of, "Come to a living Savior and a mighty Lord." They reconceive the Christian mission. Inevitably and inescapably they must do this, as it's not so much the task of introducing folk the world over to Jesus Christ the Lord, as it's a matter of going out to the other religions to enrich them. That was the nineteenth century way of envisaging the Christian mission. You take insight from the world of Christian thinking to make Buddhism into better Buddhism, Hinduism into better Hinduism, and so on.

Liberals Seek Needs

The counterpart of that, in this late twentieth century, is the reconceiving of mission in terms of *humanization*, going out in order to identify with the secular ambitions and desires and concerns of the nations and to help them forward in their desires for political liberty, economic stability, and so on. (You will know that there's a great deal of thinking of this kind in the World Council of Churches.) And all this is opposed to the preaching of the living, reigning Christ crucified and alive forevermore.

And the message is no longer presented in the terms in which Paul presented it to the Philippian jailer: "Believe in the Lord Jesus, and you will be saved" (Acts 16:31). Jesus, according to this "gospel," is an example and an influential memory in the church, but precisely not a living Savior and friend here and now in the present tense. And in the church, we have to fight the conflict constantly with liberalism, just as we have to fight the good fight against unbelief in the world.

Well, this is the situation into which these lectures of mine are being offered. What we are going to do together, God enabling us, is to rethink and to restate the essential gospel, the scriptural gospel, in the light of some of these modern trends, in the light of some of these latter-day modern movements. We are going to look at alternatives to scriptural positions; we are going to consider what can be said in favor of them and what has to be said against them. I hope we may through God's grace keep the gospel from being overlaid with misbelief in our own minds and equip ourselves to proclaim the gospel all the more clearly to others.

The Story of the Gospel

The rest of this chapter will be dedicated to the first of the series of questions that we'll be exploring. What sort of a message, what sort of good news, what sort of a communication is the gospel anyway? What sort of instruction is the word of the cross, the proclaiming of Christ crucified?

I could answer that question by saying the proclamation is essentially the declaring of a series of doctrines. I have in fact answered the question that way in print before now. If you look at my book, *Evangelism and the Sovereignty of God*, you'll find me saying that the preaching of the gospel, the message of the gospel, concerns five realities, all themes of Christian doctrine: (1) God and his holiness, (2) man and his sin, (3) Christ, his cross and his atonement, (4) faith and repentance, and (5) the Holy Spirit and new life.[2]

2 J. I. Packer, *Evangelism and the Sovereignty of God* (Downers Grove, IL: InterVarsity Press, 1971).

Putting it that way, I would be answering the question by saying the gospel is an orthodoxy. And that answer would not be false. What are doctrines? They are distillations of scriptural lines of thought for teaching purposes. The Latin word *doctrina* means teaching. As such, doctrines are, so to speak, ring fences around the reality of God at work. Creeds and confessions are similarly ring fences around the reality of God at work, and in that they consist of Christian doctrines. Within the area marked off by the ring fence, one must look, one must dig, one must explore, if one is going to grasp the truth.

Outside that area, whatever notions one finds will not be the truth. Doctrines are needed to circumscribe the truth. Doctrines are given us by God the teacher himself. Doctrines are necessary in the church because God has given doctrines to the church—God himself through his messengers has taught us the truth. Therefore, doctrines must be formulated, and doctrines must be valued. For God himself has become our teacher. What is in the Bible is doctrine and so it should be presented.

I say these things in order to convince you, if such convincing were necessary, that I am not in any sense against doctrines. In England, I find myself in many circles something of a speckled bird by reason of my enthusiasm for doctrines. But yet, what I want to say here is that to answer the question, "What sort of message is the gospel?" by saying, "The gospel consists of doctrines," would be a limited answer because doctrines as we receive them and as we preserve them and as we state them are defensive, often abstract, as formerly static. We have to remind ourselves that we are not saved, nor do we come to know God simply by being orthodox and being able to rattle off the doctrines. In my book *Knowing*

God, I make rather a song and dance about that too. That there is a difference between knowing about God and knowing God. Knowing *about* God is only the means to knowing God, just as knowing *about* a person in this world is hopefully the means of subsequently coming into a relationship with them based on an awareness and an understanding of who and what they are.[3]

I don't want to answer the question by saying, "The gospel is essentially a proclaiming of doctrines"—true though that answer would be. I prefer, for now, to answer the question like this: What sort of communication is the gospel? Answer: It's a story. It's a story told about God. Ultimately, inasmuch as it's a matter of revelation, it's a story about God told to us by God. It's a story in which God through his spokesman bears witness to himself. The theme of the story is precisely the living God at work—in this world, in the past, in the present, and in the future. It's the story of what God has done, is doing, and will do.

We've a Story to Tell

Here I note that in the Scriptures, and also in what I'm saying now, the word *gospel* is a concertina word, sometimes used with a narrower range of meaning, as when the concertina is closed up, and sometimes used with a wider range, as when the concertina is opened. Christ crucified is the heart of the matter, whether the word *gospel* is used in the narrower or the broader sense. In the narrower sense, the gospel means the area covered by those five doctrines that I mentioned just now, and the work God has done as men's Savior on the cross, and that he does in bringing men

3 J. I. Packer, *Knowing God* (orig. 1973; Wheaton, IL: Crossway, 2023).

through faith to know him now, and that he will do as he leads men on in that life that the Holy Spirit gives.

Taking the word *gospel*, however, in the broader sense that it also bears in Scripture, it signifies nothing less than the whole counsel of God, that whole divine plan that began in eternity and will only be completed in eternity. From eternity to eternity the plan of salvation will not be completed until the church is perfect in glory.

I am using the word *gospel* now in the wider sense rather than in the narrower sense, with scriptural precedent for what I am doing. The gospel, as I'm saying, is essentially a story, a narrative about God.

We may learn this way of looking at the matter from our hymns. Hymns take us again and again to the heart of Christianity. You might think that the missionary hymn, which I am just about to quote, is naïve in some ways; nonetheless, it makes this point for me admirably as I think. It is the hymn that provided the title for this chapter:

> We've a story to tell to the nations,
> That shall turn their hearts to the right,
> A story of truth and mercy,
> A story of peace and light. . . .
>
> We've a message to give to the nations,
> That the Lord who reigneth above
> Has sent us his Son to save us,
> And show us that God is love.[4]

4 H. Ernest Nichol, "We've a Story to Tell to the Nations," 1896.

Or again, with equal naïvety but with equal truth, we may look at the children's hymn:

Tell me the old, old, story
Of unseen things above
Of Jesus and His glory,
Of Jesus and His love. . . .

Tell me the story slowly,
That I may take it in—
That wonderful redemption,
God's remedy for sin. . . .

Tell me the story always,
If you would really be
In any time of trouble,
A comforter to me.[5]

The story—yes, exactly. The hymns are right. You can get the same message from the theologians. Take the late Karl Barth. In the 1920s, he was insisting already that his purpose as a theologian was to focus on the simple points of Christian truth. And in 1962, touring America for the last time, he was asked by some American wiseacre what was the profoundest thought that he'd ever had. And Barth answered by quoting from the children's hymn, "Jesus loves me, this I know, for the Bible tells me so."[6]

5 Katherine Hankey, "Tell Me the Old, Old Story," 1866.

6 Anna Bartlett Warner, "Jesus Loves Me," 1959.

The Heart of the Story

Paul wrote Romans as his great, elaborate, full-dress exposition of the gospel. And he started it almost ceremonially with a great, full-dress sentence announcing the subject of the letter. The sentence reads like this:

> Paul, a servant of Christ Jesus, called to be an apostle, set apart for the gospel of God, which he promised beforehand through his prophets in the holy Scriptures, concerning his Son, who was descended from David according to the flesh and was declared to be the Son of God in power according to the Spirit of holiness by his resurrection from the dead, Jesus Christ our Lord, through whom we have received grace and apostleship. . . ." (Rom. 1:1–5)

But I needn't read further. You see what Paul is announcing: the gospel, the good news concerning the Son—a historical personage descended from David according to the flesh, who rose from the dead—Jesus Christ the Lord. This is history. This is a story of what God has done.

And bracket with that the opening verses of 1 Corinthians 15, where Paul recalls the Corinthians to basics, saying:

> Now I would remind you, brothers, of the gospel I preached to you, which you received, in which you stand, and by which you are being saved, if you hold fast to the word I preached to you—unless you believed in vain. For I delivered to you as of first importance what I also received: that Christ died for

> our sins in accordance with the Scriptures, that he was buried, and that he was raised on the third day in accordance with the Scriptures, and that he appeared. . . . (1 Cor. 15:1–5)

Again, we have to say: This is story. This is narrative. This is history. This is a proclamation of what God has done. You don't need me to remind you that in the letter to the Romans, Paul moves from what God has *done* to what God is *doing* in giving life to those who have faith in Christ, and what God *will do* in perfecting the church. Remember how Romans 11 paints that glorious vision of the church finally complete, Jew and Gentile together in the one body and God all in all? Likewise, in 1 Corinthians 15, Paul moves from looking *back* to Jesus's death and resurrection into the *present*, the forgiveness of sins that those who believe in the resurrection have, and into the *future*, the Christian hope of resurrection someday when the trumpet sounds and the dead are raised. This is the gospel, the declaration, the story of God's work—past, present, and future.

In 1936, studying the sermons in the book of the Acts, C. H. Dodd found the apostolic preaching, the characteristic *kerygma*, recurring again and again as men proclaimed the fulfilling of prophecy in the life and death and resurrection—the present reign and the future return—of Jesus Christ the Lord.[7]

Yes, all the way through the New Testament the gospel is declared as history. Let's not dance around this word *history* as so many scholars today, alas, do. When I speak of history, I mean the space-time continuum within which you and I are found

7 C. H. Dodd, *The Apostolic Preaching and Its Development* (1936).

at ten to nine on this Tuesday evening in September 1978, and which has been continuous since the world was made. History is the public stage of that space-time continuum, and the events that we are speaking of and that the New Testament records took place within that space-time continuum. And the nature of this story can be characterized by saying, in principle: If we could travel back through time with H. G. Wells's Time Traveler in *The Time Machine* or with the modern Dr. Who in his police box, we could in principle stand with those who listened to Jesus's preaching in Galilee long ago, stand with those who watched him die on the cross, stand with the women and the disciples at the empty tomb on the third day. These things happened. And in principle if we could travel back in time, we could have shared in the events ourselves. We could have witnessed what others in fact witnessed.

It's in this simple, straightforward, basic sense that we say, these things proclaimed in the gospel are history. For the apostles themselves clearly and unambiguously so regard them. The gospel is history. It is story. It is the narrative of what God has done in the space-time continuum—and does still, and will do until history reaches its end.

A Story in Many Strands

The Bible narrates this story by ringing the changes on various key themes, which in different places of Scripture become focal points for the telling of the story. The gospel, we might say, is like a rope made up of a number of strands woven together, and each of these different presentations of the gospel is just one of those strands. But the gospel in its fullness isn't before us until all the strands have been woven together and the whole rope has been constructed.

THE STORY OF THE KINGDOM OF GOD

What, you say, are the separate strands? Well, you can tell the story first as the story of God's kingdom: of how God expressed his unchanging kingship—his sovereignty over his world—by bringing that world, following man's initial rebellion, back into actual submission to his rule once again and the actual enjoyment of the saving mercy: the gift of eternal life that those who submit to God's rule come to know.

The story begins with man's rebellion and consequent loss of spiritual life in the garden of Eden. It goes on to show how God made himself King, first over his own people Israel. It tells how he set up a monarchy to rule in his place over his people Israel, how through the prophets he established in the minds of his people the hope of a greater King—a Son of David who would be David's Lord who was later to come. It shows how his Son came into the world to be that King: Jesus, the Christ. It tells us how, following his crucifixion and resurrection, he became King, reigning in heaven at the Father's right hand and how one day he is coming in his kingdom, finally to establish in a public and open way, that dominion that is already his, albeit unacknowledged for the most part by man.

This is the story of God's kingdom and of Jesus Christ the King in that kingdom. In spelling out this strand of the scriptural message, we shall pay special attention to the history books of Scripture, all the Old Testament, to many messianic passages in Old Testament history, and to the first three Gospels in the New Testament in particular, all of which dwell on this theme.

THE STORY OF THE PEOPLE OF GOD

Second, you can tell the gospel story in terms of the theme of God's people: God is fulfilling his purpose of creating a people who shall live in fellowship with himself, worshiping him and witnessing to him, glorifying him and enjoying him both now and forever. This story begins in eternity with the three who are one resolving to have man in their fellowship, and then on the stage of time the story goes on to tell us how God chose Abram and Abram's seed to be his people. The story tells how he called Abram's family out of Egypt and in the wilderness made them his people by covenant, and established worship—the pattern of priesthood and sacrifice—to ensure that the fellowship between them should always be an experienced reality and that nothing should block it.

The story would go on to tell how he taught Israel to live in fellowship with him. The story continued through to Jesus Christ, the true Israel, the seed of Abraham and his own person in whom Israel is reconstituted. The story would go on to show how the New Testament church is in fact the new and true Israel in Jesus Christ. And the story would end with spelling out the nature of the new community that God by his grace has brought into being: the church as the people of God, the church as the body of Christ, and the church as the community of the Spirit. The church is the third race in this world, the international society with a heavenly life. The church is the company of those who know the forgiveness of sins, fellowship with God by grace through faith, and eternal life now.

For the telling of the story in this way, we should draw most heavily on Exodus and Deuteronomy and Hosea in the Old

Testament, and books like Galatians and Ephesians and Revelation in the New Testament.

THE STORY OF THE MEDIATION OF GOD

In connection with the general story of God creating a people, we should tell, as perhaps a part of it or a separate theme, the third strand in the gospel story: the story of mediation, that is, the story of God's special work of grace to create fellowship between sinners and himself.

We should tell the story of how God first set up a typical priesthood and sacrifice and place of access in order to teach his people that there was a need for mediation. We tell how the pattern of mediation came finally to be fulfilled in Jesus Christ, who is both our great high priest and the one perfect sacrifice for sins for all God's people for all time. We must tell them of Jesus, who by his sacrifice has substituted for that tabernacle, followed by the temple in Jerusalem, the particular locality where men were told to worship God. The situation, the state of affairs, is one in which any man, at any time, may call upon God through Jesus Christ, and find himself in Christ's presence with his mediation effective. We tell how he is bringing them to God and keeping them in fellowship with God. This is the story of mediation.

The pattern is spelled out in Exodus and Leviticus, and the reality is spelled out in the Gospel of John and Galatians and Romans and most of all in Hebrews, where we are shown how Jesus fulfills in his own person and by his sacrifice this pattern, this picture of mediation. So then this third strand in the gospel story is that of God's initiative in mediation, whereby he brings sinners into fellowship with himself.

THE STORY OF THE VICTORY OF GOD

A fourth strand in the gospel story is the theme of renewal—both the renewal of the world and the renewal of a disordered creation. Creation is morally disordered through the revolt of Satan and the consequent revolt of men, and cosmically disordered, as Paul indicates without going into details in the middle of Romans 8. But disorder has not come to stay. This strand of the gospel message proclaims that Satan and his adherents, both angelic and human, are doomed. Their revolt cannot last forever. Satan is a defeated foe. He will be judged, and those who side with him will be judged. By contrast, those who put their faith in God through Christ are already being inwardly renewed in heart and spirit and character. One day they will be outwardly renewed and given bodies to match in resurrection. On that day, the whole cosmos will be renewed. There will be a new heaven and a new earth, and the glory of God will finally and fully be shown forth throughout the cosmos as the waters cover the sea.

This way of telling the gospel story is a proclamation of divine victory, by stages, over sin and the disorder that sin has created. For telling the gospel story in this way, the passages of special relevance are Genesis 3, Romans 8, much in Isaiah, 2 Peter 3, much in Revelation, and so on.

THE STORY OF GOD THE FATHER GLORIFYING HIS SON

Fifthly, you can tell the story as the story of the glorifying of God's Son. You can announce it and present it in terms of the Father's purpose to honor and make known his Son as co-Creator, as

Redeemer, as head of the church, as the source of life to sinners, as the world's present Lord and coming King, and as the one who men are to worship and honor as they honor the Father. Looked at from this standpoint, the gospel becomes an invitation to bow down and worship Jesus Christ. The Scripture passages especially relevant for telling the story in this way are the Gospel of John and the letter to the Colossians and again much in the book of Revelation.

THE STORY OF THE IMAGE OF GOD

Sixthly, one can tell the story as the proclamation of the perfecting of man in God's image. One can tell the story in terms of man, and the problem that he raises and that he presents to himself, and in terms of the solution that God, the God who made him, provides to that problem. Who am I? Why am I here? Whence did I come? Where am I going?

God's answer, revealed in the gospel, is that every man was made to be God-like. Every man was made to live in the image of God and in fellowship with God. I believe that biblical theology teaches us to see the image of God as destiny, no less than endowment. It was both the one and the other.

As for image as endowment, we see man made in the image of God in Genesis 1. The image consists of rationality (the capacity to make plans and carry them through), creativity, dominion, spiritual knowledge, knowledge of divine reality, and with that righteousness and holiness. I can prove all those things, I think, from Genesis 1. Surely it is right exegesis and theology to understand the image of God in Genesis 1, first and foremost, in terms of the presentation of God in Genesis 1, and in that chapter, rationality, creativity, dominion, knowledge, and holiness are the qualities that God in Genesis 1 is shown as manifesting.

But man's destiny was to live in a way that exhibited godlikeness every moment, and in every activity, for the whole of human life. And in that sense, likeness to God was man's destiny. Of course, Adam fell and so his destiny wasn't fulfilled. But the New Testament picks up the theme and proclaims the image of God as restored in Christ through union with Christ. Union with Christ is another of the great gospel themes. In Ephesians 4:24 Paul spoke of the gospel as a summons to put on the new man, which is created after the "likeness of God"—the image of God, we might say, for that's what likeness means. Man is created after the image of God "in true righteousness and holiness." Similarly, Colossians 3:10 speaks of Christians as having "put on the new self, which is being renewed in knowledge" of God and all that that entails "after the image of its creator."

Everything that the New Testament has to say about God's gift to man in Christ, about the holiness that he requires, is in truth part of the theme of restoring in man God's image as his destiny. This is yet another strand in the gospel story, yet another way in which that gospel story can be told.

The Man Christ Jesus

The Humanity of Jesus Christ

[illegible] Galilean Jew crucified probably in AD 30. [illegible] was [illegible] died [illegible] [illegible] [illegible] is something [illegible] [illegible] -century [illegible] who [illegible] was a [illegible] apart from a tiny handful [illegible] scholars—e.g., [illegible] *The [illegible]* ([illegible]) and G. A. Wells, *Did Jesus Exist?* (1975) [illegible] believe that he never existed.

What Sort of Man Is Jesus?

The question [illegible]: [illegible] the New Testament, [illegible] the Gospels and the Epistles, particularly Paul in [illegible] and Hebrews [illegible] in other words, [illegible] man whose true identity [illegible] he was God's eternal Son? [illegible] the real Jesus a [illegible] who [illegible] not [illegible] described [illegible] [illegible]

2

The Man Christ Jesus

The Humanity of Jesus Christ

JESUS, CALLED CHRIST, was a Galilean Jew crucified probably in AD 30. As noted in chapter 1, that he was not a mythical figure but a historical character and certainly a man, is something nobody has ever doubted since the first-century Docetics, who thought that he was a theophany, apart from a tiny band of scholars—e.g., Arthur Drews, *The Christ Myth* (1909) and G. A. Wells, *Did Jesus Exist?* (1975)—who believe that he never existed.

What Sort of Man Is Jesus?

The question presses: Was he the sort of man that the New Testament, both the Gospels and the Epistles, particularly Paul in Colossians and Hebrews 1, tell us that he was? Was he, in other words, a man whose true identity was that he was God's eternal Son? Or was the real Jesus a person who should not be described in those terms? That's a question pressed by a number of folk within the Christian church at the present time. One might have expected it to be pressed constantly by folk outside. It's a little more surprising when it's raised inside, and we must face it.

I want first to make a comment on the nature of the Gospels, where the person of the man Jesus is presented to us, as we see him walking to and fro, we hear him speak, we watch him at work.

Second, I am going to offer you a very brief and inadequate summary of New Testament faith concerning the person and place of this man Jesus.

And thirdly, I shall offer you a review of what is called humanitarian Christology, that is to say, the alternative view of the person of Christ that is offered by those who doubt the propriety of calling him the Son of God. They speak of him, this man, as at most, a uniquely Spirit-filled man, a prophetic man, a remarkable and outstanding man, but when you've said that, according to them, you've said it all. They have effectively reduced the incarnation of the Son of God to a special case of the indwelling of the Spirit in a man, just that. We'll review the humanitarian Christology and see how it works.

The fourth thing I'll do, to close, is offer you a presentation of the humanity of Jesus as set forth in the letter to the Hebrews, where it seems to me a series of points of crucial relevance are made for our instruction.

1. The Nature of the Gospels

I plunge straight in with my initial comment on the nature of the Gospels that present this man to us. As in general, the New Testament is a confession of faith written by believers in Jesus for believers in Jesus. In particular, the four Gospels were written by men who held the faith of the Epistles concerning Jesus in order to help others enter more deeply into the faith of the Epistles concerning Jesus. That is a thesis I don't think can be controverted. The gospel, in the sense that Matthew, Mark, Luke, and John are Gospels, was a new literary form corresponding to nothing that had existed before. It was so called quite plainly because the selection of narratives of Jesus's words and deeds—which each writer presented in the course of his book, and then the elaborate passion story to which the introductory narratives led—were carefully calculated presentations of the good news. These stories were intended, just when taken together in their plain natural sense, to add up to a presentation of the gospel of Jesus. And because the four writers believed that that was what their narratives did add up to, they called their works the Gospels.

This is very obvious in fact in John's Gospel where you have a didactic prologue to start with. You have interpretative comments by the apostle at many key points in the story as it goes along, and you have of course elaborate doctrinal discourses as part of the Gospel, discourses in which all these things are made very plain indeed from the lips of our Lord himself. What you have in John is thus what we might call old-fashioned storytelling, in which the author makes a point of seeing that the moral of his tale, the meaning of the story that he's narrating, comes out very clearly.

By contrast, the Synoptics—Matthew, Mark, and Luke—tell their story in what we might call the modern manner. They narrate without comment; they hope and indeed plan to make their impact on the reader simply by their arrangement of material and by the buildup of the storyline as the narrative develops. These first three Gospels are as far as possible from being artless memoirs as the critics of two generations ago urged that they were. No indeed, they are carefully wrought theological documents, in which all the details of the storytelling have been carefully shaped and angled in order to force upon the reader's notice the particular presentation of the gospel which is Jesus—or shall I say the particular presentation of Jesus as the gospel with which each writer is concerned. Matthew presents him as the Savior King. Mark presents him as the Servant of God who makes atonement. Luke presents him as the perfect man who is also God's perfect and final prophet. And John tells the story in his more old-fashioned manner, rounding it all off by presenting him as the Son of God incarnate.

The recognition by scholars that each of the evangelists had his own special purpose of this kind, and shaped and selected and angled his narratives to that end, has produced a new critical technique, which the scholars have added to source criticism and form criticism, the two techniques they have been using for many moons now in their study of the Gospels. The new technique is called redaction criticism. It's emerged into the light of day in the past twenty years. It's precisely the study, so far as the Gospels enable to discern this, of how each evangelist angled, shaped, and selected, in the telling of history, in order to get his own particular message across.

It's a sad fact that just as source criticism and form criticism have been pressed into the service of skepticism, the service, that is, of the supposition that in the course of transmission the facts concerning Jesus have been falsified, forgotten, and then reconstructed imaginatively in a way that puts the narratives right out of step with what really happened—so redaction criticism has been pressed into the service of skepticism. Books by redaction critics have gravely explored from all sorts of angles the question of how far the evangelists felt at liberty to twist the traditions and falsify the facts in order to make their own theological points.

There is in fact no good reason whatever to believe that this was what they did. As a writer of books myself, I make bold to say to you, it is part of every author's responsibility to present the facts that he selects so that their meaning, at least what he takes to be their meaning, will be most clearly understood by the readers.

And redaction criticism is the study of how the evangelists fulfilled authorial responsibility. Is that responsibility compatible however with falsifying the facts in order to make a point? It is not thought so today.

There is no reason to believe it was thought so in the first century AD. Is there, however, reason to believe that the evangelists labored to be faithful in the witness they bore to the historical Jesus? Yes, indeed there is. At the end of John's Gospel and at the beginning of Luke's Gospel are claims and attestations to the fact that what is being read in these books can fairly be taken as truth, for it's based on knowledge and faithful witness. And until that approach and until that assurance rather proves impossible to accept, we must as rational students accept it as our working hypothesis.

That doesn't mean that the concern that the redaction critics have to explore the precise ways in which the evangelists have shaped their stories so that they might be better understood should be discounted. No indeed—it's very helpful in the study of the Gospels to pursue it. I have been a redaction critic since the time before redaction criticism was invented. I mean, the time before the word existed. I was a redaction critic, I now discover, as long ago as 1949, when I heard a senior New Testament scholar read a paper to a learned society in which he sought to explain Luke and the passion narrative entirely in terms of a scissors-and-paste hypothesis of what Luke was doing with his sources.

And I ventured in discussion to suggest that the shape of the story as we have it might rather be due to the particular theological emphases that Luke saw in the story and wanted his readers to pick up from the story. And lo and behold, the day after, I was visited by the late professor R. H. Lightfoot, who had been sitting in the meeting and who had himself begun to explore this line of thought, now called redaction criticism, as long ago as 1936. And to my utter amazement, he spoke to me as though I was virtually a prophet, because in fact I'd been speaking along the lines of his own study.

Of course, it's grown familiar to all evangelical Bible students. We know, simply from careful attention to the text, that each evangelist had his own angle and his own emphasis, and that he selected and arranged his material in order to bring out his own emphasis. There's really nothing new for us in this point at all. Why then, am I laying such stress on it? Well, simply in order to provide myself a foundation for saying this: That when one reads the Gospels as presentations of the gospel, one finds that in the case of all four, the purpose of the narrator is exactly as stated explicitly, by John in 20:31: "These are written," says John, "so that you may believe that Jesus," the man, "is the Christ, the Son of God, and that by believing you may have life in his name." And this proves on inspection to be wholly in line with the gospel, the Christological message of the whole of the rest of the New Testament.

2. Jesus in the New Testament

It is very striking to see though how the various New Testament books—and I am thinking now of the Epistles rather than the Gospels, which are simply narratives—use many different concepts, many different ways of expressing the truth, but nonetheless all converge on the same point, precisely the point that these words that I just quoted from John are making. Jesus is the Christ, the Son of God, and these things we proclaim in order that believing, you who hear us, you who read us, may have life through his name.

And that leads me to the second thing that I said I would do. I want to offer you, as pointedly as I can, a summary of New Testament faith as a whole, concerning the person and place of the man Christ Jesus. I'm very conscious that I have to oversimplify here. I'm very conscious that I'm doing little better than cartooning, leaving out from my picture many subsidiary details and highlighting, perhaps overstressing, the key points simply in order to underline them. That's what cartoonists do. But if you think that cartooning is a valid art form, perhaps you will be patient with me for the next section, as in my simple cartoonists' style, I summarize the New Testament faith concerning the person and place of Jesus.

Essentially, it seems to me, the New Testament teaching on the person of Jesus reduces to four points like this.

a. Jesus Is the Messiah

Jesus of Nazareth is God's promised Christ, the long-foretold Messiah. The Greek word *chrīstós* represents the Hebrew *mašîaḥ*. Messiah, is not of course a surname like Dumbrell or Packer or

Knox. It's something far more significant than that. It's an office title, as our Presbyterian friends would say. It means literally "the Anointed One." It designates God's promised Savior-King. That the Galilean rabbi who was crucified and rose from death is the Christ, God's long-prophesied Messiah, was always the basic Christian conviction, and all strands of the New Testament express it.

The revelation of Jesus as the Christ—the demonstration of it, you might say—is the plot of the Synoptic Gospels. The announcement of it is the main theme of the sermons in Acts. The explanation of it is one of the main themes of the Epistles.

As a matter of fact, the Messiah's fulfillment of his earthly ministry, in face of incomprehensible hostility, right up to his dying and his rising, is the storyline of all four Gospels. That Jesus's own mysterious title for himself, *Son of Man*, and equally the title *Lord*, given him from Pentecost onward, are titles that point first to the reality of his Messianic rule is something nowadays generally agreed in the world of scholarship.

Not that Jesus's concept of messiahship corresponded to Jewish expectation. His notion of Messiahship reflected his view of God's eschatological kingdom, which he preached as a reality that his own ministry brought into being, and he saw that kingdom in a way in which no previous Jewish teacher had seen it, namely, as a new relationship between penitent sinners and God as their heavenly Father, a relationship that was achieved through commitment to himself in faith as their sovereign Savior. He saw his own lordship in the kingdom as based on his call to be God's suffering servant, the innocent one who having died for others' sins is then vindicated by being restored to life according to Isaiah 53.

Calvin well summarized Jesus's notion of his own messiahship, and with it the overall New Testament view of the Messiah's role, when he spoke of Jesus as fulfilling the threefold office to which men were anointed in the Old Testament: the office namely of *prophet*, bringer of messages from God; *priest*, offerer of sacrifice to God; and *king*, ruler of the people of God. And all those three offices as one comprehensive office fulfilled in his own personal ministry, in his life, and in his risen reign.

In the proclamation of Jesus of Nazareth as the Christ is bound up a claim that is at the heart of Christianity: Jesus, the man of Galilee, is central and essential to a true understanding of history. For according to Old Testament prophecy, God's Messiah and the kingdom in which he reigns—the Son of David reigning in a kingdom greater than that of David—this kingdom and this reign is the center of world history, the heart of it, the moment of supreme significance, that which gives meaning to everything else. And it's the New Testament witness with one accord that this has become reality through the coming of Jesus of Nazareth.

So this is the first strand in the New Testament faith turning on the person and place of Jesus. Jesus of Nazareth is the Christ, and this is what Christhood, his messiahship, means. And then a second thought: Jesus of Nazareth, says the New Testament, is the unique Son of God.

b. Jesus Is the Son of God

Granted, there are places in the first three Gospels, and in Acts too, where Son of God may be no more than an honorific title for the Messiah, modeled on Psalm 2:7 and following, where you remember God says (and this was originally said, it would seem, to Israel's king), "Thou art my Son; this day have I begotten thee" (KJV). But it's certain that in the Epistles and in John's Gospel, Son of God signifies a unique relation of solidarity with the Father, a relation entailing both a revelatory function and also a share in the Father's work of creating, sustaining, reconciling, ruling, and renewing the world.

For the revelatory function of Jesus the Son of God, think of John 1:18: "No man hath seen God at any time; the only begotten Son, who is in the bosom of the Father, he hath declared him" (KJV). That's what the Greek verb is literally expressing, the thought that Jesus offers us an exegesis. The Son has offered an *exegesis* of the Father. The only begotten Son has expounded him.

For his share in the Father's work of creation and redemption, think of the opening sentence of the letter to the Hebrews: The Son, in and through whom God has now spoken to us, being the brightness of God's glory and the express image of his person and the one through whom he made the worlds—when he had himself purged our sins, sat down at the right hand of the majesty on high (cf. Heb. 1:1–3) There is solidarity in the work of creation and redemption.

And certainly there are places in the first three Gospels where the witness Jesus bears to his knowledge of his own unique filial identity in relation to the Father is very plain indeed. For instance, in just one text of many, he says, "All things have been handed over to me by my Father, and no one knows the Son except the Father, and no one knows the Father except the Son and anyone to whom the Son chooses to reveal him" (Matt. 11:27; Luke 10:22). Jesus sees himself as the Son, the only one of its kind. And of course the witness of the voice from heaven, heard at the baptism and the transfiguration, bears the same testimony, "This is my beloved Son" (Matt. 3:17; 17:5). The lexicography of that word translated *beloved* suggests uniqueness as part of the meaning.

Certainly, personal distinctions within the unity of the godhead constitute perhaps the hardest notion around which the human mind has ever been asked to wrap itself, and the thought was never adequately conceptualized until the fourth century. But faith that Jesus was in the true sense the Son of God made flesh, and therefore to be worshiped, marked Christians out from the start.

There is here too a central claim that Christianity makes, a claim namely that Jesus Christ, Jesus the Man of Galilee, is central and essential to a true understanding of God as well as to a true understanding of man. Perfect and ideal Man indeed he is, but that's not the whole of the story, nor perhaps the first part of the story. The first part of the story is that in this Man, we see in person God come to save. And if we are going to think Christianly about God, we must start from the axiom so well-formulated by Michael Ramsey in the three simple words: "God is Christ-like," for Jesus is God.[1]

This is the second strand in the New Testament witness to the man Christ Jesus: He is the Messiah (that's his office), and he is the Son of God (that's his personal identity).

c. *Jesus Is the Only Way to the Father*

That leads on to the third claim that the New Testament makes about Jesus of Nazareth: he is the only way to the Father—the only way whereby we may come to know God the Creator as

1 Arthur Michael Ramsey, *God, Christ and the World* (London: SCM Press, 1969), 98.

Father and stand related to him as Father, so that we may know ourselves as children in his family. Here is a key theme of Jesus's own teaching, of Paul's teaching, and of John's teaching. Upon it, we may say at once, is based the crucial Christian claim that it's only through Jesus of Nazareth that we may have true understanding of God's love.

The New Testament views the knowing of your Maker as your Father, and the knowing of yourself as his child and heir, as being the highest privilege and the richest relationship of which any human being is capable. Not to know God in this way, however, is to be in a state of fallenness and guilt, to be cut off from God's life, to be exposed to his judgment, and indeed to be living under demonic control from all of which flows only misery. Yet this is every man's natural condition, says the New Testament. Can it be changed, we ask?

Jesus is reported as answering that question in the affirmative by saying this: "I am the way, and the truth, and the life. No one comes to the Father except through me" (John 14:6). It is as if he said, "Yes, a filial relationship to God is possible through being related to me and to my mediatorial ministry—but not otherwise."

Sonship to God, in the sense that guarantees me in glory, is not a fact of natural life but rather a gift of supernatural grace. John, in one of his expository comments in the prologue to the gospel, states it in these terms: "To all who did receive him, who believed in his name, he gave the *right*"—the power, the privilege—"to become children of God" (John 1:12). The doctrine of the bestowal of sonship then is part of the proper exposition of 1 Peter 3:18, "Christ also suffered once for sins, the righteous for the unrighteous, that he might bring us to God." Bring us to God, understand, as children. Bring us to God as God's own adopted sons. The only begotten Son who died for us presents us to his Father as his brothers and sisters, and thus we are adopted into the family, and we sinners, taken as it were from the moral and spiritual gutter, become children in the royal family.

Jesus is thus the way—the only way—to know God as Father. The true understanding of God's love has to do with the recognition that "God so loved the world, that he gave his only Son, that whoever believes in him should not perish but have eternal life" (John 3:16), the eternal life that involves not only forgiveness of sins, not only fellowship with God in a broad and general sense, but quite precisely, adoption into the royal family and life as God's sons and heirs, objects of his special adopting love.

And as no other relation to God, save sonship, brings the salvation to which God's children are heirs, so apart from Jesus, who effects our adoption, there is according to the New Testament, "no other name under heaven given among men by which we must be saved" (Acts 4:12). Claim number three is an exclusive claim: Jesus of Nazareth is the only way to the Father.

d. Jesus Is the Only Hope

The fourth claim, the final point, is this: Jesus of Nazareth is the only hope for any man. Hopelessness, as the Bible knows and as we today know, is hell, literally. As God made us to fulfill a function and attain an end, for "man's chief end is to glorify God and enjoy him forever" (as the Westminster Shorter Catechism puts it), so he made us creatures for whom hope is life. And whose lives become living deaths when we have nothing good to look forward to.

As the deep hopelessness of this post-Christian Western world tightens its chilly grip on us, we are made to feel this increasingly in our day, and so we can better appreciate the infinite value for our lives of that exuberant, intoxicating, energizing hope of joy with Jesus in the Father's presence, which is so pervasive a mark of New Testament Christianity.

Men without Christ are there declared to be without hope. But Christians are declared to live already in a light that brings hope and that shines brighter until the perfect day. They know, as Paul puts it, "Christ in you, the hope of glory" (Col. 1:27). It's a pity I think that we hear so little in these days about what has well been called "that unknown world with its well-known inhabitant," to which the New Testament teaches Christians to look forward. For as the hymn says, "The Lamb is all the glory of Emmanuel's land," and the hope of Emmanuel's land is part of the glory of the gospel.[2]

So here is the fourth strand, under which the New Testament witness to Christ may be expanded, the strand under which the hope of the Lord's personal return of course must be subsumed as a very prominent element in the exposition of it. Jesus of Nazareth the coming King is the only hope for any man. And on these four claims, on this fourfold testimony to the person and place of Jesus, on this declaration that he's Christ and Son of God, and the way to the Father, and man's true and only hope, there rests classical Christian Christology as set forth by Chalcedon and classical evangelical preaching too, for it's only on this basis that we are warranted to say Christianity is Christ and are warranted to tell

2 Anne R. Cousin, "The Sands of Time Are Sinking" (1857).

folk that being a Christian is a matter of a personal encounter and a personal relationship with this personal divine Savior.

This is the line of teaching to which I suppose you and I are accustomed, and this is a line of teaching which perhaps we never thought that folk within the church would question. But it is questioned. And now we must turn to look at the line of thought that questions it and pass in review the humanitarian Christology that offers itself as an alternative to acceptance of this New Testament witness to the Savior.

3. Jesus in the Modern Humanitarian View

I offer you now—again I'm afraid in simplified, perhaps oversimplified, perhaps cartoon terms—a rundown of humanitarian Christology as exhibited for instance in a book like *The Myth of God Incarnate* or Maurice Wiles's *Remaking of Christian Doctrine*. My concern is not so much to engage with any particular exponent of it—there are a number of exponents of it, all telling the story in slightly different accents—but rather to show you how this hypothesis, viewing it generically, works.

The Bible: Reliability and Reconstruction

It has the same generic shape and works in the same basic way in the minds of each of its expositors. We begin with two *a prioris*, two things that the theologians who take this line assume and treat as granted.

The first is that the Bible, in particular the New Testament, is a book of religion, a testament of experience and faith rather than a written revelation from God. Because its status is only that it is a testament of faith, it is not necessarily reliable, either in its facts or in the meaning it gives to the facts that it records. There is nothing necessarily definitive about its teaching, just as there is no necessary accuracy, no necessary truthfulness, attaching to the details of its witness.

And *a priori* number two is this: reconstructions of the past that do not involve the supernatural, the miraculous, and the unique, are preferable to those that do. This includes the Christian past, that section of the past that deals with Christian origins, and with that explanations of the evidence concerning Christian origins that we find in the New Testament books.

Here are the two *a priori*s that operate as springboards to start this hypothesis off. On the basis of these two *a priori*s, the scholars feel at liberty first to separate the figure of the Jesus of history, whom they seek to reconstruct, from the Christ of faith in the New Testament. They feel themselves at liberty, in other words, to question whether the Christ of New Testament faith does faithfully represent what the Jesus of history really was.

And secondly, they allow themselves to separate that which they can regard as natural. I mean the ethical teaching and the moral and spiritual example of the Lord Jesus from that which they regard as supernatural in the stories. I mean the record of his miracles and his resurrection and indeed his incarnation, the incarnation of the Son itself.

They allow themselves to press the question: Must we include these supernatural elements in our reconstruction of the Jesus of history? Do we have to say more about him than that he was a good, godly, spirit-indwelt man who gave teaching of unique value and set an example of unique significance? And out of that sort of questioning comes the hypothesis that we label humanitarian Christology, which generically runs thus: Jesus was in fact precisely a prophetic man, God-indwelt, speaking words such as no man had ever spoken before, living a life of a quality that no man had ever matched before. But he was supernaturalized by his followers. Because they so revered him for his teaching and for the power of his life, they ascribed miracles to him, they ascribed deity to him, they proclaimed that he rose from the dead. They persuaded themselves that he had done so, that he must have done so. But the truth about him corresponds to the view of the Greek gods, put forward by the fourth-century Macedonian philosopher Euhemerus, that they were men worshiped after their deaths. And, says this hypothesis, so it is with Jesus.

The supernaturalizing of Jesus, so these scholars affirm, was a development influenced and shaped by Hellenistic mystery religions, all of which had at the heart of them some myth about some god and some promise of contact with that god. And say the scholars, this same pattern of thinking was taken up by the Christian theologians and it produced the developed theology, Christology, which our New Testament gives us.

But the truth is that New Testament theology and the Christian tradition that has followed it, in deifying Jesus and making him the Mediator, and so setting him apart from us as unique in his own person, made a great mistake. And the gospel must be reconstructed so as to eliminate this mistake. The truth of the matter is that Jesus was a uniquely godly man, uniquely guided, enlightened, led by the Holy Spirit, whose significance for us is this: that he was, in a wonderfully inspiring and indeed life-transforming way, a teacher of godliness and an example of godliness whom one cannot contemplate without being changed.

It's in this way that these theorists seek to preserve the Christian sense of the uniqueness of Jesus. It's not that he is the Son of God incarnate. It is that he lived a life of uniquely potent quality, which makes a uniquely strong and uniquely transforming impact on those who come in contact with it.

Jesus: Man or Myth?

That's the hypothesis, generically. It is spelled out, in slightly different terms from chapter to chapter, by the different essayists who contributed to the book *The Myth of God Incarnate*. As we said in the first chapter, the word *myth* in that title means an imaginative story—not a matter of public objective space-time fact, but a product rather of the creative imagination—that gives an understanding of the world and of our existence in it. And that, according to the scholars, is the special significance of myth. It gives understanding of the world and our existence in it. The myth of the incarnation, say these men, was devised in order to try and spell out in terms the sense of being transformed down to your roots, which had come to Jesus's first disciples in virtue of their contact with him and, in the case of their first converts, their knowledge about him.

That word *myth* then is not intended to degrade Jesus in the mind of these men. It's intended rather to point to the fact that New Testament theology is supremely concerned with the impact that the figure of Jesus made on those first disciples and can make still. And, say the authors, the New Testament still has some value because it continues to mediate that impact. But if we ask the authors of the myth what really the Jesus of history was, well, they say different things. John Hick for instance says that he was one of the many saving manifestations of the cosmic divine *Logos*. But, says Hick, what we must do with him is bracket him with the Buddha and other great religious teachers of history. And now I quote him. I don't want you to think I'm doing anything but quote him, though the quotation may take your breath away when you hear it.

This is what he writes, "What we cannot say is that all who are saved are saved by Jesus of Nazareth."[3] So much for Acts 4:12 then, which I quoted earlier: "No other name under heaven given among men by which we must be saved."

Maurice Wiles expounds the matter this way. He believes that the man Jesus still operates as the focal point of God's mystical revelation to the soul, God's pressure on the soul, whereby he convinces us that he is there and that he has goodwill toward us and toward all men. Maurice Wiles appears to be a kind of a deist, and that's all the doctrine of God that he really has. But he believes that that sense of things is mediated through Jesus. And so he writes, again I quote, "The truth of God's self-giving love and the role of Jesus in bringing that vision to life in the world would remain," even if the doctrine of the incarnation were abandoned, as Wiles urges it should be.[4]

So much then for 1 John 4:10, where the apostle explains his statement "God is love" in these terms, "In this is love, not that we loved God but that he loved us and sent his Son to be the propitiation for our sins." Apparently not. But still the message of God's love comes through, according to Wiles.

3 John Hick, *The Myth of God Incarnate*, ed. John Hick (London: SCM Press, 1977), 181.

4 Hick, *The Myth of God Incarnate*, 9.

The most robust thinkers in fact at this point in the *Myth* book are Don Cupitt and Dennis Nineham, who seem to be saying that Jesus's significance for us is like the significance of George Stephenson in the *History of Railways*: Jesus was the one who set it all going. He set going the experience of God that is transmitted by contact down the ages in the church. But his significance apparently is only historical, and for us who live in these latter days, not direct any more than a person designing a railway system today would go back to study George Stephenson before he allowed himself to decide how he was going to do it. Well, alright. I make those quotations not in order to guile their authors but simply to show you how this Christology works out in terms of the question that we all want to ask: What then is the importance of Jesus for us today?

The New Testament: Fact or Fiction?

What should we say about this type of thinking, this humanitarian Christology? I don't want to question for one moment the sincerity or the erudition of its exponents, though I do think they are assuring themselves rather obviously to be men of their time, pre-possessed by some fashionable modern prejudices that have determined the way they think.

However, I would point out to you first what surely is obvious to us all, I need not spend time on it. This is a total destruction of apostolic Christianity, and it leaves us with no Savior of the kind that the New Testament presents. Second, I would point out to you this view appears to involve what one can only call an arbitrary disregard of evidence. On this I must spend a moment in order to make the point. It's a point that has three branches.

First, in this twentieth century, scholars such as James Denney, Sir Edwyn Hoskins, Oscar Cullmann, Professor Charles Moll, Professor A. M. Hunter, Professor F. F. Bruce, and many more have demonstrated, in a way that seems to me very cogent indeed, that transcendent claims made by Jesus for himself are there in the earliest Synoptic material. However early you go, by the use of accepted critical techniques in your analysis of material in the Gospels, there still you find Jesus of Nazareth claiming an allegiance, which only God has a right to claim, and claiming that allegiance on an exclusive basis as part of man's service of God.

If you accept the hypothesis, which seems to be gaining ground in these days, that the Gospel of John is early rather than late, well there is abundantly more material of the same kind in John's Gospel, and the earlier date at which you put that Gospel, the harder it is to believe that any of this material is in the least authentic.

Second, John Robertson's book, *Redating the New Testament*, has made the point, not indeed that the whole New Testament was written before AD 70 (that he cannot prove and does not suppose himself to have proved) but that it is arbitrary and unnecessary to suppose that any of the books of the New Testament were written after AD 70.[5] So it is arbitrary to embrace any theory that presupposes a late date for any New Testament book as part of its foundation and that could not stand unless that late date were assumed.

If you are going to assume that Jesus had been so comprehensively misremembered, or shall I say forgotten, and then reconstructed, prior to the writing of the New Testament, as this

5 John A. T. Robinson, *Redating the New Testament* (London: SCM Press, 1976).

humanitarian Christology assumes, you have to allow much more than a generation for that process to happen. There simply isn't time for it to happen prior to AD 70. The proof of the fact that it couldn't have happened before AD 70 is that here am I a man of fifty-two, quite able to remember the Second World War well, which broke out in 1939. Many of you I'm sure can remember it too, and the time interval is exactly the same, just under forty years. This is a point that tells very strongly against the humanitarian Christology.

Third, New Testament Christianity from the historical standpoint is simply inexplicable, save on the basis that there was an empty tomb. There were appearances of the risen Lord and many did know his personal presence with them in those early days. It's a rule of historical thinking that you must posit a cause adequate to the effect. The effect that you are seeking to explain here is lives transformed and men willing to live and die in order to bear witness to the resurrection of Jesus. It seems to be unsound historical reasoning to suppose that any cause could have produced that effect save an empty tomb, resurrection appearances, and the sense of Jesus's presence through the outpouring of the Spirit, which in fact the narrative of Acts says was the thing that was there at the start.

On the principles of humanitarian Christology, however, there was no physical resurrection. Any resurrection appearances that men thought they saw were hallucinatory, have to be, and where the sense of Jesus's presence came from is anybody's guess. It is a rather forlorn hypothesis, don't you agree, on which to explain the revolutionary, transforming, dynamic effect of early Christianity? So I think we do not surrender our intellectual integrity by being deeply skeptical of the skepticism of the humanitarian Christologists.

4. Jesus: Son and Savior

That leads me briefly to the last thing that I want to say: just a quick word about the presentation of the humanity of Jesus in the letter to the Hebrews, which I want you to contrast with the presentation of the man Christ Jesus in the humanitarian Christology. How does Hebrews set forth the man Christ Jesus? Why like this? By affirming two propositions. First, that the preexistent Son of God took flesh and blood and became man and that this is the real secret of the identity of Jesus. This is who he is. And second, that the purpose of the Son of God in taking flesh and blood was to save his brethren.

In other words, the letter to the Hebrews affirms incarnation, and incarnation as a means of saving ministry. In the first two chapters, incarnation is affirmed. God brought his "firstborn into the world," says the writer in Hebrews 1:6. In chapter 2, he quotes Psalm 8, "What is man, that you are mindful of him?" And having quoted Psalm 8, he goes on to say, "Now we don't as yet see all things made subject to any man, but we do see Jesus." How does Jesus come in? Why, Jesus comes in as the Man in whom this pattern of dominion is fulfilled archetypically through his saving ministry. We see Jesus, "who for a little while was made lower than the angels, namely Jesus, crowned with glory and honor because of the suffering of death, so that by the grace of God he might taste death for everyone" (Heb. 2:9).

We read a little further. Who was this Jesus? Why, he was the Son of God who took to himself human flesh and blood in order that he might draw men to himself and bring them to glory as his own brethren, sons of God in the family in which he is the elder brother. It says in verses 14–15, "Since therefore the children share in flesh and blood, he himself likewise partook of the same things, that through death he might destroy the one who has the power of death, that is, the devil, and deliver all those who through fear of death were subject to lifelong slavery." The Son of God took to himself flesh and blood and did so in order to save.

You don't need me to remind you how the letter to the Hebrews goes on to spell out his saving ministry, in terms of high priesthood, and to spell out the nature of high priesthood, in terms of the godward ministry of offering sacrifice. He the High Priest offered himself, and in terms of the manward ministry of help, sympathy, guidance, and support, grace to help in time of need.

You don't need me to remind you how the epistle to the Hebrews sets before us our one high priest on high, his atoning work done, now ever living to make intercession for us and able to save to the uttermost those who come to God through him. Having been tempted, he's able to help them that are tempted, and through his intercession to secure for us grace to help in time of need.

This is the presentation of the man Christ Jesus in the letter to the Hebrews. He is the Son of God made flesh. He took to himself flesh and blood in order to be our great high priest, in order to save. Were there no incarnation, according to Hebrews, there would be no mediation and no salvation either. So indeed there is "no other name under heaven given among men by which we must be saved" (Acts 4:12).

Let me sum it up quickly. The gospel set forth in the Gospels, and in the New Testament as a whole, presents the historical figure of Jesus as the divine Savior. We preach Christ crucified, says Paul. This is history, and the Christ who was crucified is the Son of God. We have looked at the humanitarian Christology, which views Jesus as simply a man indwelt by God, which as I said reduces incarnation to the indwelling of the Spirit. And we have seen that it leaves us with no gospel at all—no gospel at least that is recognizable as a gospel by New Testament standards.

We have also suggested that the humanitarian Christology is unreasonable, as well as being un-evangelical and in every sense un-Christian. We are left where the New Testament leaves us, with the conviction that in stating the gospel, it is right and necessary to shine the Christology of the Epistles as a light, a lamp, to illuminate the man, the figure, Jesus of Nazareth who walks through the gospel story. This Christology, this declaration of the Son of God made man, shows us who that Jesus is, explains everything about him. He indeed made the claim, but the Christology of the whole New Testament spells it out. And as we see that figure, illuminated by this declaration of who and what he is, so we shall find again and again as Christians before us have found, that he steps out of the pages of the Gospels and becomes the living Christ, the living Savior, whom we know and whom we love, and whom we acknowledge as our Friend, because he has come to us and made himself known to us. And we worship him, and we love him. He is our God, he is our brother, he is our Master, he is our Lord, the one true Christ of New Testament witness.

Well, it is for us, if by God's grace we have known this in our own lives and are able with the centurion at the cross, perhaps with more understanding than the centurion at the cross to say, "Truly this was"—and is—"the Son of God" (Matt. 27:54).

3

He Emptied Himself

The Divinity of Jesus Christ

LET ME BEGIN BY REMINDING YOU where we've gone to so far in this course of study. My lecture course was announced as a series of contemporary studies in the eternal gospel. And my overall purpose in these five sessions is vindication and restatement of the old, true, apostolic gospel in the face of questions, uncertainties, and alternatives that are being canvassed at this present time. I took the phrase from 1 Corinthians 1, "We preach Christ crucified," as Paul's way of summing up the gospel. As a very convenient text for my own restatement of the gospel, what we are seeking to see in these five studies of different aspects of the gospel is the full meaning and the deeper implications of "Christ crucified" as a summary of the gospel message.

The Story: Christ Crucified

In the first chapter I made the point that the phrase "Christ crucified" points to the central fact in a many-stranded story about the living God in history saving men and ultimately renewing this whole world order. I urged that the gospel is story. It is history, not a product of the human imagination. The gospel is significant because as a story, it gives understanding of ourselves and of our lives. It is precisely revealed truth taught by God, taught by God to the apostles, through the Holy Spirit, given to them and taught by the Holy Spirit, through the apostles to us via the written testimony of the epistolic writers in the books of the New Testament.

And in the New Testament, though different categories and vocabulary are used by different persons—the witness to the gospel, the witness to Christ crucified at the heart of the gospel—proves on inspection to be one. Themes converge. The message is a single message. The message is that the historic cross—AD 33 was probably the year it took place—is an event of trans-historical significance, and indeed of trans-historical reality. The New Testament obliges us to affirm boldly that folk who come to faith in Christ are touched directly by the cross and by the resurrection involved in it.

According to Paul's line of thought in Romans 6, "We have died with Christ." We are raised with him. We come to be involved in that central momentous event of God's plan for the renewal of his world. Part of the message is that the Christ who died and rose and who now touches our lives is in truth the living Lord. He's *there*, in the sense in which Francis Schaeffer spoke of *The God Who Is There*. As the Christ who is there, he's *here*, very present to bless those who turn to God through him. He reigns. He will come again. He will bring in the new heavens and the new earth in person. He is the living Lord, with whom one day all men will have to reckon, for one day all men will meet him as Judge. He is the living Lord, whom the gospel now invites us to receive as Savior, the Christ who was crucified on Calvary's cross so long ago.

So we began to counter the suggestion that the New Testament theology should be understood as myth. We continued to counter that suggestion in our second study, when we looked more closely at the so-called humanitarian Christology, which is precipitated out of the world of thought, which begins in the minds of many of these modern teachers with an insistence that New Testament theology has the nature of myth.

The Savior: Christ Jesus, the God-Man

When the smoke has cleared away, what the humanitarian Christologians are left with is a Jesus who was a prophetic man, indwelt by the Spirit, living a life of unique godliness and unique power to influence those who came in contact with it. But his significance for us is precisely that of an example and a teacher, not the significance of a sin-bearer, not the significance of a risen Lord, not the significance of a mediator to be worshiped, not the significance of a friend to be loved.

There is no objective atonement, according to these men, any more than there is an objective resurrection. We looked at this view, and we saw that it represents a denial of the New Testament message rather than an interpretation of it, which is what its own proponents claim. We saw that it does not fit at all the historical evidence concerning Jesus and Christian origins. It flagrantly disregards that which is the united thrust of the New Testament theologians. When they speak of Jesus, they mean namely this, that the clue to understanding him is to realize that he is, in truth, the Son of God who took flesh and blood and was made man in order that he might save man. The New Testament insists that the humanity of the Son is integral to his ministry of mediation and redemption in the sense that had he not been man, he could not have done what had to be done in order to save us.

And we saw the writer to the Hebrews spelling that out in terms of his key category of our Lord as the great high priest appointed by God to have both a godward and a manward ministry—a godward ministry of making sacrifice for man's sins. And this great high priest of ours offered himself his own blood as the sacrifice for our sins.

And then on the other hand, the high priest's ministry is to sympathize with, understand, and so help men in their needs and their troubles, and only a fellow man, says Hebrews, can do that. So the high priest had to be human as well as divine. The humanity of Jesus Christ is now seen as part of the mystery, the glorious mystery of divine action for our redemption.

This brings us to the subject of this third chapter. What we're going to do is examine a hypothesis about the incarnation, which is offered indeed not as a challenge to the Bible account of Jesus Christ, the Son of God, in the way that the myth hypothesis was. Instead, it is rather offered as an attempt to explain certain features about the incarnation.

I shall begin by setting up a danger sign and warning you against speculations. Second, I shall prepare our minds yet further for the theory we're going to examine, by illustrating a little further from the New Testament its declaration of Jesus's divine identity. There are two passages that we shall briefly look at. Then thirdly, we'll examine this hypothesis, the so-called kenosis theory of the incarnation. I shall round off with a brief remark under my fourth heading, offering a final comment on the divinity of Jesus and the gospel.

The Speculations

We begin with a discussion of speculations. There are two things that I want to say here. It's very important that, as we approach the study of so high and holy a mystery as the incarnation of our Lord, we should make this point to ourselves and make it very clearly. It's a point which I make by the two statements following.

1. Theologians should not trust speculations.
2. Theologians must form hypotheses.

First, theologians should not trust speculations. I'm using the word *speculation* here in a quite precise sense. I mean by it, an educated guess that goes beyond the Bible. I think it very important that we should realize that all we can know about God in his own nature and in his plans and his purposes and his redemptive action is what the Bible tells us.

Beyond that we creatures are in no position to penetrate by guesswork. Martin Luther once had to chide Erasmus, who was a speculative theologian. The rebuke took this form. "Oh, Erasmus," said Luther. "Your thoughts of God are too human."[1] If we allow ourselves to speculate beyond the Scripture concerning the redemptive purposes of God, well, the same thing for sure will have to be said of our thoughts too. We shall, without realizing it,

1 *Martin Luther on the Bondage of the Will: A New Translation of* De Servo Arbitrio *(1525): Martin Luther's Reply to Erasmus of Rotterdam*, trans. O. R. Johnson (J. Clarke: 1957). The introduction was written by J. I. Packer.

make God in our image. We shall, without realizing it, assimilate him, our Creator, to us, his creatures. And that will be a mistake. And the thoughts that involve that mistake will be mistaken all along the line.

No, what we must do is recognize that we are shut up to learn of God in his redeeming action from the Scriptures. And the business of theology is to echo the Scriptures, to confess the faith of the Scriptures by circumscribing and articulating the mysterious realities of which the Scripture speaks. Again, when I use that word *mysterious*, or when I use the corresponding noun *mystery*, I'm using the words in a quite precise sense. I am referring to a reality of which we know from Scripture and of which, we have to say (as we have to say of just about all the divine realities revealed in Scripture), we can be sure that it is so because the Bible tells us so. But we cannot conceive how it is. At that point, we have to confess that the reality transcends our understanding. We know *that* it is; we don't know *how* it is.

The realities of God, all of them, are *incomprehensible* (to use the technical word again). They are above us, above our reason—not unreasonable, no indeed, but transcending reason. And our knowledge of them can only be partial as we follow the Scriptures, the Scripture teaching, and embrace it and assimilate it and make it part of our own thinking while we grasp truth. Our knowledge of these things is indeed true as far as it goes, but we can be sure that it's incomplete, as with all our knowledge of these divine realities we have to say, "Now we see in a mirror dimly"—obscurely, imperfectly, and incompletely (1 Cor. 13:12).

That doesn't mean that we have to be skeptical or agnostic. No indeed. For what we do know, because God has shown it and told it to us, is amply sufficient for a fully satisfying relationship with God, as indeed Christians have known right from the very beginning of Christianity. One can illustrate that by saying that in a human family, the father can be a genius, an Einstein, and his son maybe is only three or four years old and won't begin to grasp all the profound thoughts that are buzzing in his father's mind. But nonetheless, the boy could have a perfectly fulfilling loving relationship with his father, if his father loves him and cares for him as a good father will. And similarly, we can know God in love and fellowship, even though we do not know and cannot know all the things about God that God himself knows about himself.

When one thinks of the great doctrines of Christianity—the Trinity, the attributes of God, his sovereign providence, the incarnation, the atonement, union with Christ in death and resurrection—we see this straightaway. First of all, we only know anything about these things from the Bible. And second, we only know these things in part. There are many questions, that is, that we can ask about them that we aren't able to answer. We only know what the Bible tells us, and that means that these things remain mysteries to us in the sense defined. Speculations are attempts to think about these matters beyond the bounds that Scripture sets and beyond the sure ground that biblical thinking gives. Calvin, on the subject of predestination, laid it down at the beginning of his treatment, that one must not go a single step beyond the clear teaching of Scripture or else one will get giddy and fall into the abyss.[2]

2 John Calvin, *Institutes of the Christian Religion*, III.21.1.

And what Calvin said of predestination can be said, I think, of all the mysteries of God with which the Scripture deals. If we speculate beyond what the Bible actually says, we get dizzy. We fall into the abyss. So I warn you, brothers and sisters, as I warn myself: theologians should not trust speculations.

But the balancing truth is this: theologians must form hypotheses because this is how theological knowledge is extended. There's a parallel here with scientific method. In generalizing on the basis of the data available, what scientists do regularly, each in his own field, is to go beyond the data in forming a hypothesis that is a notion of how it might be a conception of what possibly is true.

And then having formed a hypothesis, the scientist proceeds to test it by seeing whether it squares with all the data that he's got at the moment, and whether he can find other data that tends to prove it. It is similar in theology. Theology is a science. Theology is the study of the revelation of God. Theology, too, is the gaining of knowledge, in this case from what God has said. Theologians form hypotheses concerning the great realities of which Scripture speaks, and then test those hypotheses by asking questions of Scripture, to see whether the Bible does in fact speak in a way that accords with the hypothesis or whether it speaks differently.

Only as you put hypotheses to the test in this way can you discern whether in fact they do clarify and crystallize Scripture truth, or whether they have in fact no better status than that of speculations, which the Scripture won't support. Hypothesis as such is not a speculation until it has been tested and until you have discovered that the Bible won't support it. If you hang onto it then, speculation indeed is the proper name for it, and you've made a mistake in your methods and are abusing your own mind.

That the theologian mustn't do. But he'll only get on as he forms hypotheses and tests them out.

I say this because we are going to consider one such hypothesis, and it is not illegitimate to form it, nor illegitimate to try it out. The question is whether it's wise to hang on to it when, as we shall see, there proves to be so little scriptural support for it.

Christological Identity: Eternal God

But more about that in just a moment. I wanted to bring before you yet more of the New Testament evidence concerning the deity of our Lord Jesus Christ. I want to show you precisely, from these two passages that I'm going to quote, how the New Testament—in its witness to the fact that Jesus is to be honored and worshiped as the Father is honored and worshiped, for he indeed is co-eternal with the Father and shares with the Father and has shared with the Father in the work of creation just as now he is with the Father in the work of redemption—focuses specifically on the thought of the Savior's preexistence as the second person of the Godhead, who was there with the Father before he became Man. I want to show you this first from the prologue to John's Gospel, John 1:1–18. I shall not be attempting to offer you a full exegesis of this passage, but I do want to show you how the thought progresses within it.

Its thrust isn't always appreciated even by the best commentators. We should understand it, I urge, like this. The aim of the prologue is to introduce the person and the ministry of Jesus Christ, the Son of God. John's special concern throughout the Gospel is to show us first who and what Jesus was and, indeed, is. This is a concern to show us his glory as the Son of God, and to show us, secondly, what is the nature of the grace and the truth that he brought—to show us the nature of Christ's salvation.

And he has a problem. He wants to make sure that none of this is misunderstood. He wants to ease into our minds—clearly, unambiguously, and right at the start—the notion that the person of whom he is speaking is the Son of God in the full Christian sense of that phrase, the sense which he wants to expound. And he wants us to understand that it is, in truth, a divine person who came to bring us that grace and that truth that saves. He knows that the phrase, "Son of God," in the minds of many of his readers, will convey immediately something a great deal less than what it conveys to his mind as a Christian teacher. He knows that to Jews, "Son of God" is a phrase that need be no more than an honorific title for the Messiah.

To the Gentile, the phrase "Son of God" will suggest most likely one of these heroes of Greek mythological legend, who had a human mother and a divine father. And he doesn't want to allow anyone for one moment to think that Jesus Christ, the eternal divine Son, is like, say, the hero Hercules or someone of that sort.

So he doesn't begin by speaking of the Son of God. What he does is to begin his prologue with the section, thirteen verses long, of which the theme in a phrase is this: "Meet the cosmic divine Logos." The word *logos* means argument, reason. When logos is translated *word*, that's the thought that lies behind the translation. "Meet the cosmic divine Logos," says John, and then he tells us straight away certain things about the Logos.

He's eternal. "In the beginning was the Word" (John 1:1).

From eternity he was in communion with God. "The Word was with God" (1:1).

Eternally, he was divine himself. "The Word was God" (1:1).

He was the Father's agent in creation. "All things were made through him" (1:3).

He is the immediate source of life, in all its forms in this world that God has made through him. "In him was life, and the life was the light of men" (1:4).

He, the Word, the Creator Word, came "into the world," John continues (1:9). His coming was heralded by John the Baptist.

Despite this, he was widely rejected. When he came, he came to his own people. He came to his own world, and his own people received him not. Those who did receive him, however, were blessed. He gave them the right, the privilege, the honor of becoming the children of God, those namely "who believed in his name" (1:12).

Now these things are all being said of the Logos, the Word. And as these wonderful and momentous things are said about the Word, John is calculating that the interested reader will be asking with increasing urgency, "Who is this Word? I never heard of this Word before. Who is he?"

Then, from verse 14 to verse 18, John answers that question by telling us who the Word is. And if the heading that sums up the thrust of the first thirteen verses was the heading, "Meet the cosmic divine Logos," the heading for verses 14 to 18 is, "Meet the Father's incarnate Son." In verse 14, you come to the watershed, the momentous point in the preface at which the identification is made.

Look how it's done. "The Word became flesh" (1:14), simple words with such profound meaning. "The word became flesh and dwelt among us, . . . full of grace and truth. We beheld his glory"

(1:14). Glory, of course, is a word that speaks of the manifested presence of God. "We have seen his glory, glory as of the only Son from the Father" (v. 14), glory given by the Father to his only Son. That's the thought. And from this moment onward, we hear nothing about the Word. From this moment onward, John talks consistently about the Son.

"Meet the Father's incarnate Son," he says. "That's who the Word is." The Word, remember, is divine, co-eternal with the Father, the Father's agent in creation, the Father's agent in bringing children into the family, the agent that is in redemption. This Word is the Son of the Father. And so one must think of him.

And throughout the rest of the Gospel, we are taught to do so. "The Word became flesh and dwelt among us, and we have seen his glory, glory as of the only Son from the father . . . from his fullness we have all received, grace upon grace. For the law was given through Moses; grace and truth came through Jesus Christ" (1:14, 16–17). There, for the first time, is his human name. And this is who Jesus Christ is: the Son of the Father, whose glory we saw. You see the connections; you see the identifications. The Word is the Son. The Son is Jesus Christ. And now we are tuned in to the theology of the Gospel of John. Now, John, with wonderful skill, using simple words, has told us quite unambiguously who and what the man Jesus Christ is.

The preexistence of the Word who is the Son is the point at which the story starts. I highlight this because the preexistence of the Son in personal fellowship with the Father from all eternity has been challenged by some of our wise, modern Christologists. It's a disastrous point to challenge, however. It's an essential point to affirm. If it's challenged, if it's lost, then immediately the truth of the Trinity has been abolished. That surely is plain, and you are shut up once more to the humanitarian Christology, which sees Jesus as a God-indwelt man and denies the true incarnation, in such a book as John Robinson's *The Human Face of God*.[3]

There is deep confusion here, for Robinson challenges the personal preexistence of the Savior, and yet Robinson believes that he's being loyal to the historic, Trinitarian, and incarnational faith of the church. It's the same confusion, in fact, as ran through his *Honest to God* fifteen years ago. It's a very dangerous and damaging and destructive confusion indeed.

Christological Identity: Suffering Servant

But there it is. John's Gospel is perfectly clear and explicit. And so is the second passage to which I want to refer you here: Philippians 2:5 and following, that famous hymn, which Paul probably did not write (no one can be sure about that) but which certainly he makes his own by working it into the text of his letter to the Philippians and making its declarations part of his own argument.

"Have this mind among yourselves, which is yours in Christ Jesus," he says in verse 5. Incidentally that translation, which is the Revised Standard Version, is, I'm sure, correct. It is not: "Have this mind among you, which *was*, or which *you see*, in Christ Jesus." No, the only natural way to render the Greek is, "Have this mind among yourselves, which *is yours* in Christ Jesus"—wrought in you already by virtue of your recreation through the Holy Spirit, in his image. Now express it, says Paul.

3 John A. T. Robertson, *The Human Face of God* (Philadelphia, PA: Westminster Press, 1973).

"Be who you are." And that's the thrust of the passage. And at this point he launches into the hymn.

> Have this mind among yourselves, which is yours [which is instinctive to you, one might almost say] in Christ Jesus, who though he was in the form of God, did not count equality with God a thing to be grasped [something to grab and hang onto seems to be the notion], but emptied himself, taking the form of a servant, being born in the likeness of men. And being found in human form he humbled himself, and became obedient unto death, even death on a cross. (2:5–8 RSV)

It's a model of humility, giving yourself in a costly way for the sake of others. The word translated *form*, in the phrase "form of God," signifies a form that is an appearance, a set of outward characteristics, which are a true clue, a genuine index to the nature of the thing whose form it is.

These two items in front of me have the form of a microphone. Why so? Because they are microphones, so it would be appropriate, if I were speaking Greek, for me to use the word *morphe* when I say these two objects have the form of microphones. And when it's said that "he was in the form of God," *morphe* means the same. He was God. This is the implication of the phrase.

But for all that he was God, he emptied himself and took on him the form of a servant. Those two phrases expound each other, for eternal God not to count equality with the Father a thing to grab and hang on to, but to take to himself the form of a servant is for him to empty himself of dignity and of glory and of honor. That's what the phrase means.

And so Paul goes on to explain that he was born in the likeness of men and being found in human form he humbled himself and went down even lower and became obedient unto death. Well, I mustn't stop on this passage. All that I want to do really from it is to underline the fact that it begins with an assertion of the preexistence of the Son. That's where the story starts. He was in the form of God, but from there, he came down.

That phrase, however, he "emptied himself" at the beginning of verse 7 has already I'm sure made your minds move forward to think of the kenosis theory, which builds so much, or has in the past built so much, on that phrase. And to the kenosis theory we must now move without more ado.

Christological Identity: Incarnate Son

Let us examine the kenosis theory as a hypothesis about the incarnation to see how it measures up to the witness of Holy Scripture. Whence came this theory? It originated with a group of nineteenth-century Lutherans, and then from a number of English-speaking theologians who took up the Lutheran notion. Bishop Charles Gore, the pioneer liberal Catholic theologian in England, picked it up, first in his essay in the book *Lux Mundi*.[4] Men like the Presbyterian theologian H. R. Mackintosh, and the Congregationalist theologian P. T. Forsyth, and the Methodist theologian Vincent Taylor have also taken it up in more recent days. It's really a Trinitarian speculation as you'll see, or Trinitarian hypothesis, shall I say, not to anticipate my verdict.

4 Charles Gore, ed., *Lux Mundi: A Series of Studies in the Religion of the Incarnation* (1889).

The Theory

What Is the Kenosis Theory?

The kenosis theory is an account of the divinity of the incarnate Son throughout his earthly life. What is the theory? It's an assertion that the deity of the incarnate Son, the deity of the man Christ Jesus, was reduced deity, "shrunk deity" I will allow myself to say, throughout his earthly life, in consequence of a pre-incarnate decision whereby the so-called metaphysical attributes of omnipotence, omniscience, and omnipresence were put in abeyance for the period of the incarnate life. How exactly they were put in abeyance is explained differently by different theorists; we needn't bother with that for the moment. Suffice it to say that that's the general idea, so that the Son of God who was born into this world and whose human name is Jesus was never at any time omnipotent, omniscient, or omnipresent.

So, whereas the Christian tradition sees Jesus Christ as God-plus, that he's the Son of God and the fullness of his powers acquiring through the incarnation a capacity for all forms of human experience without any diminishing of his deity. And whereas the humanitarian Christology says that Jesus was man-plus—man plus the indwelling, the anointing, of the Holy Spirit, though he had no divine identity at any time.

The kenosis theory says that Jesus Christ is God plus *and* minus. *Minus* certain capacities that have been his before, but *plus* all these new capacities for human experience as orthodox Christology affirms. And indeed the suspicion that underlies the kenosis theory in all its exponents is that Jesus could not have entered fully into certain aspects of human experience, had he not laid aside these divine powers in his glory before he took human nature to himself.

Why Do People Consider the Kenosis Theory?

I anticipate the answer to the next question I raise: Why have men taken up with this theory? What has led them to it? The first answer to that question is that they believe that this hypothesis accounts for certain phenomena in the Gospels, which it's not easy to account for on any other terms, e.g., the limited knowledge that the man Jesus showed at certain points.

I illustrate from the question he asked in the story recorded in Mark 5:30, the story of the woman with the hemorrhage who crept up in the crowd and touched him and was in fact healed through touching him. And Jesus stopped and asked the question, "Who touched my garments?" And the natural way of reading that is to suppose that at the moment of asking, he did not know. Bishop Gore wanted to develop it in this way: Jesus, in his view of the nature of Scripture, was no better and no different from any educated Jewish theologian of his own day. He assumed, for instance, the traditional authorship of Psalm 110, which he quoted as the word of David, "The Lord said to my Lord: 'Sit at my right hand, until I make your enemies your footstool.' "(Luke 20:42–43). But, said Bishop Gore, we know perfectly well that this is a Maccabean psalm dating from the second century BC, and not written by David at all. And so we must realize that from this bit of evidence that Jesus simply didn't know, and at this point was, shall we say, the victim. Well, these phenomena and others like them, so it's urged, are best accounted for by the supposition that the Son in his glory, the

Son whose human name is Jesus, had laid aside his omniscience before he became man.

Furthermore, the second reason for embracing this theory: it is argued that only on this view could Jesus have entered into all the experiences of limitation that are part of what it means to be human. To know the limits of one's own knowledge; to know the limits of one's own power; to know that though one would like to be somewhere else at this present moment, one can't be. Had not the Son abandoned omnipotence, omniscience, and omnipresence, well, he would not have known that limitation as being an integral part of his life—and this, so it's urged, is part of what it means to be human.

And thirdly it's urged by the exponents of this theory that the thought of the Son actually freezing, abandoning, parting from divine powers in this way gives more substance than ever to the thought of the great love and the great condescension that he showed when he became man for our salvation. It brings out, so they urge, part of the dimension of meaning in 2 Corinthians 8:9, "He who was rich, yet for your sake he became poor, so that you by his poverty might become rich."

Is The Kenosis Theory Biblical?

I ask a third question. Now we begin to test the hypothesis. Is there any Scripture for this? Is there any direct biblical assertion of anything like this? Here I think our answer has to be no. As we saw a moment ago, Philippians 2:7 (he "emptied himself") is concerned with the abandoning of divine glory and dignity and honor, which was involved in the Son's taking to himself the form of a servant to fulfill the pattern of Isaiah 53.

And 2 Corinthians 8:9. "He was rich, yet for your sake he became poor, so that you by his poverty might become rich," is similarly speaking of the Savior, coming down to earth in order to live as a poor man and die as a poor man, become an outcast and an outlaw in the society of his day. But there is no biblical assertion of the abandoning of the metaphysical attributes.

Indeed no biblical statement that I can find shows the slightest interest in any such idea, which shows that any such notion had never crossed a Bible writer's mind. No, this is a speculation.

Is the Kenosis Theory Necessary?

I now raise a fourth question. Is it not in fact a very awkward speculation, raising many new questions to which no good answer can be found and actually solving none, when one looks at it again? I ask, is it not very audacious, this theory, in what it ventures to say about the psychology of God incarnate, the man Jesus? Granted, he did experience human limitations, no question about that. But is it really necessary to posit that he knew he couldn't know more than he did, that he knew he couldn't do other than he was doing, and so on and so forth for him to have entered into those experiences?

WHAT HAPPENED TO DIVINE OMNISCIENCE?

I'm going to suggest in a moment that it was not so necessary. I'm going to offer you in a moment an alternative hypothesis, which I believe to be more scriptural, concerning those occasions when our Lord declared that he did not know certain things. But for the moment I limit myself to asking the question: Isn't it audacious to affirm that he must have known that he couldn't?

There were certainly things that he knew he could have done and didn't do. Matthew 26:53 is an example, "Do you think that I cannot appeal to my Father, and he will at once send me more than twelve legions of angels?" But I'm not doing that, says our Lord. But I'm not going to. Is it really necessary to suppose that in the case of our Lord's not knowing certain facts, that the same doesn't apply? We'll return to that in a moment.

WHAT HAPPENED TO THE TRINITY?

Let me ask another question. Isn't this speculation audacious in the way that it envisages the life of the divine Trinity? What happened, we ask, to the cosmic functions of upholding the universe, which he brought into being by the word of his power, those cosmic functions which are attributed to the Son of God in a number of the theological passages of Scripture? One in Colossians 1, one in Hebrews 1, and so forth. What happened to the universe while the Son was on earth, devoid of his omnipotence and omniscience? The late Archbishop William Temple pressed this criticism. He says, in terms of a theory, what ought to have resulted would have been cosmic chaos.

Vincent Taylor believes he knows the answer to that one. Surely, he says, the resources of the Trinity would be able to deal with this particular problem. But that's just a high-flown phrase, a pontifical-sounding phrase that conceals this thought, which I deliberately put in a colloquial way in order to bring it right down to earth: That there was an agreement between the Father and the Son, or perhaps the Father and the Spirit and the Son, that the Father and the Spirit would take on the Son's job while the Son was away.

Well, I know that when, for instance, a person like myself is away from college, a colleague may take some of my lectures for me, but I must say, I think it's very audacious. It goes far beyond any scriptural warrant for supposing, but similar things happen within the unity of the three in one. I think this is a mythological fantasy if ever there was one, and I don't for myself buy it.

WHAT HAPPENED TO THE DUAL NATURE OF CHRIST?

Isn't this notion open to the criticism of being monophysitism in reverse? Do you know that word, *monophysitism*? It's a heresy. It's the heresy that the Savior had only one nature and not two. Doesn't this theory so maim the Savior's deity that you cannot say that he was fully divine during his life on earth? I ask the question.

WHAT HAPPENED WHEN CHRIST RETURNED TO HEAVEN?

I ask fourthly, isn't this hypothesis actually self-negating in this way: The supposition is, that in order to enter into the fullness of human experience on earth, the Son must renounce some of his divine powers. Question: What happens when the Son returns to glory? The kenosis theorist is now confronted with a dilemma.

He must say one or other of two things. Either he must say this: that the Son regained those metaphysical attributes, which hitherto he'd been without, in which case, the problem arises at once. How can he be? How can his experience in glory be truly human? Or else he has to say that in as much as the Savior's experience always continues truly human, he never gets those metaphysical attributes back at all. Forgive my down-to-earth language, but I believe that this is a dilemma on the horns of which the kenosis theorist is inescapably impaled. I want to put it to you in a way, which makes the point—or shall I say the points of the horns—just as sharp as possible.

I think that it's in the interests of clarity to do that. Neither horn of the dilemma seems to me to be in the least acceptable on kenotic principles, though since I don't recognize the problem that the kenosis theory purports to solve, the dilemma doesn't touch me.

IS THERE A BETTER EXPLANATION?

Let's try now to be positive and constructive. Isn't there a better explanation than the kenotic one of the limitations—the limited knowledge, for instance—that Jesus showed in the course of his earthly life? I believe that there is. To prepare the way for what I'm going to say, I ask you to remember that though there were times when Jesus showed professed ignorance of facts, there were also times when he exhibited supernatural knowledge—as when, for instance, he saw Nathanael under the fig tree; when he foreknew Judas's betrayal and spoke about it very freely in John 13 and elsewhere; and when he told the woman of Samaria that he knew all about the five husbands that she'd had, although he'd never met her before. These facts also have to be explained.

The explanation that we give must account for them, as well as for the ignorances. Now I search the Scriptures, and I read passages like this. Two words from the Lord himself, the first in John 6:57, "I live because of the Father." And again, his word in John 5:19, "The Son can do nothing of his own accord, but only what he sees the Father doing." I ask, may not these words give a clue to the way that we should understand our Lord's testimony to limited knowledge when he was on earth? I suggest to you that the clue for understanding this is the reality of his dependence on the Father's will, for at every level he acts in eternity as the Father's agent in creation, and then in upholding the world that he's made, and acts in time as the incarnate Son calling things to mind, or doing whatever corresponds to our mental act of calling things to mind. Knowing things, I mean, and acting on what he knows. I suggest to you that it's entirely congruous with the whole of the rest of the Scripture witness to the Son's dependence on the Father for the whole of the life that he lives. That the Son should not know, that is, should not have in mind what the Father does not will at that moment that he should have in mind.

In Mark 13:32, we have the confession of ignorance that has caused perhaps the sharpest debate. Jesus is talking about the time of his return. And he says, "But concerning that day or that hour, no one knows, not even the angels in heaven, nor the Son, but only the Father." Are we to explain that in terms of the abandoning of omniscience by the Son prior to incarnation, or are we to explain it in terms of the Son knowing that it's not the Father's will that he should have the date in his mind and therefore not having it there? Just like that? The immediacy and completeness of Jesus's dependence on the Father's initiative for his thoughts and his words and his acts is something that surely must be accounted another of the mysteries of the Godhead, a reality that we confess without being able fully to comprehend.

But that it is so, that there is this total dependence, seems to me to be witnessed to by a great deal in the Gospels. So I offer you this as an alternative explanation of the fact that there were times when

Jesus did not have in mind things that the omniscient Father certainly knew. I recommend what I'm saying on the ground that amongst other things, it accounts for those times when the incarnate Son did know and declare things that no one had told him and that therefore you have to say he knew supernaturally. Both the supernatural knowledge—and the awareness that it was not the Father's will that he should have knowledge—came from the same source.

In both cases, one sees the Son knowing and doing what is the Father's will that he should know. This I believe is a better explanation of the data, which prompted this theory in the first instance. I think too, that I can suggest a better answer to the question concerning the cosmic functions of the Son of God during the time of the incarnation. Here again, I confess that I'm offering you only a hypothesis, which you may think speculative. Nonetheless, it seems to me that it's preferable to that which the canonists work with. It's a hypothesis that goes back at least to Athanasius. It's argued by Archbishop William Temple vigorously among the moderns. And he's not the only one.

It is this: that when the Son of God became man, his life—his conscious mental, personal, active life—was conducted, as it were, temporarily at least, from two centers of consciousness: one cosmic, one not. One incarnate, that is to say, so that he was, to use the phrase that Calvin used, and expounding notion, "completely incomplete in the flesh and complete outside the flesh, *totus incarnate, totus extra carnate.*" It was indeed the Son continuing to uphold all things by the word of his power, but not as part of the personal mental life of Jesus Christ of Nazareth. You may think that altogether too speculative, and I can't prove it. I could only point to the fact that there's nothing in the picture of Jesus in the Gospels to suggest that part of his mental life had to do with the act of upholding of all things from where he was, so to speak, in Galilee at that time.

Divine Mystery

Well then, I will very happily settle for the position that you will have to take, namely, that this is a complete mystery, and we would be wise not to make any attempt to understand how it could be. Just acknowledge from Scripture that it is and leave the matter there. But if it's a matter of speculation for speculation, I urge that this older hypothesis works better than does the kenotic one that we aren't bound to accept either.

Well, this is the upshot of my examination of the kenosis theory. It is not proven by Scripture. It is speculative. It's a speculation that creates new problems and leaves old problems unsolved. It's a speculation, which I urge we cannot regard as satisfactory or pleasing at all, quite apart from the handle that it gives to the skeptics who want to make use of it to outflank our Lord's testimony to the divine character of holy Scripture, a very big point, surely, for all evangelical people.

Divine Love

My argument is now at an end. I close with a simple rounding-off remark about the divinity of Jesus and the gospel as presented to us in the whole coherent witness of the New Testament. From the New Testament, I wish to affirm as I close the rightness of the motive of those first kenoticists, that at least there was something in which they were right.

They wanted to magnify, to glorify, to highlight the love, the divine love that was shown in the incarnation and the cross of the Son of God. In that they were absolutely right. The Bible always points to the cross as the measure of the love, both of the Father and of the Son.

The message of Christ crucified is a message of unbelievable divine love—unbelievable except that it's real—manifesting itself in incredible self-humbling and self-giving for our salvation. And I am bold to say this: much more objectionable than what I believe to be the kenotic misconception is the humdrum, matter-of-fact acceptance of the incarnation on the cross, of which I fear some of us are guilty. That humdrum, matter-of-fact acceptance of it, I mean, whereby we just put a mental tick against it. "Yes, that's true. That's fact." And we can think about it, and we can pass to and fro in our thinking alongside it.

4

A Wonderful Exchange

The Work of Jesus Christ

HOW SHOULD WE EXPOUND the cross today, in the face of a perplexing variety of views that are put forward concerning the personal work of Jesus Christ? We've been thinking in our first three lectures about the person of the Savior, but tonight we are going to think about his atoning work. And I take as title for the lecture that phrase, "a wonderful exchange." I take it directly from Martin Luther. It seems to me that it's a superb phrase, in fact, to describe what we are talking about, what Paul was concerned to teach us about when he spoke of Christ crucified. Here is a quote from Luther, which shows you how he used the phrase.

A Wonderful Exchange

Luther writes:

> This is the mystery which is rich in divine grace to sinners: wherein by a wonderful exchange our sins are no longer ours

> but Christ's and the righteousness of Christ's not Christ's but ours. He has emptied Himself of His righteousness that He might clothe us with it, and fill us with it. And He has taken our evils upon Himself that He might deliver us from them . . . in the same manner as He grieved and suffered in our sins, and was confounded, in the same manner we rejoice and glory in His righteousness.[1]

Let's have a little more from Luther as he explains first what he conceives happened to Jesus Christ. Here he is expounding Galatians 3:13, "Christ redeemed us from the curse of the law by becoming a curse for us." This is the first stage in the wonderful exchange as Luther understood the matter. I quote him again:

> All the prophets did foresee in spirit, that Christ should become the greatest transgressor, murderer, adulterer, thief, rebel, and blasphemer that ever was or could be in the world. For he being made a sacrifice for the sins of the whole world, is not now an innocent person and without sins . . . Our most merciful Father . . . sent his only Son into the world, and laid upon him the sins of all men, saying: Be thou Peter that denier; Paul that persecutor, blasphemer and cruel oppressor; David that adulterer; that sinner which did eat the apple in Paradise; that thief which hanged upon the cross; and briefly, be thou the person which hath committed the sins of all men: see therefore that thou pay and satisfy for them. Here now cometh the law and saith: I find him a sinner. . . . therefore let him die upon

1 Martin Luther, *D. Martin Luthers Werke* (Weimer, 1883), 5:608.

> the cross. And so it setteth upon him and killeth him. By this means the whole world is purged and cleansed from all sins and delivered from death and all evils.[2]

First Stage: Substitution

That's exuberant talk, but you can see what Luther means. Luther is expounding what we call substitution, Christ in our place. Calvin, in sober and more guarded language made the same point when in his *Institutes*, he expanded those words of the creed, "Crucified under Pontius Pilate." Here he is, commenting on Jesus's trial before Pilate. I quote Calvin:

> "When Jesus was arraigned before a judgment seat, accused and put under pressure by testimony, and sentenced to death by the words of a judge, we know by these records," that is by the record of these things, that he played the role or fulfilled the role "of a guilty wrongdoer . . . we see the role of sinner and criminal represented in Christ, yet from his shining innocence it becomes obvious that he was burdened with the misdoing of others rather than his own. This is our acquittal, that the guilt which exposed us to punishment was transferred to the head of God's Son."[3]

And again Calvin says, "At every point, he substituted himself in our place to pay the price of our redemption."[4]

2 Martin Luther, *A Commentary on St. Paul's Epistle to the Galatians*, ed. Philip S. Watson (London: James Clarke, 1953), 269–71.

3 John Calvin, *Institutes of the Christian Religion*, II.16.5.

4 Calvin, *Institutes*, II.16.7.

Second Stage: Reconciliation

And now here is Luther again, speaking of the second stage in the wonderful exchange. He's writing a pastoral letter to a friend of his, George Spenlein, who was in trouble of spirit, who had written Luther a very sad letter expressing his sense of grief and distress and alarm because of his own continued sinfulness. Luther wrote back to him in these terms:

> Learn Christ and him crucified. Learn to praise him and, despairing of yourself, say, "Thou Lord Jesus, art my righteousness, and I am thy sin. Thou has taken upon thyself what is mine, and has given to me what is thine. Thou has taken upon thyself what thou was not, and has given to me what I was not."[5]

And that, according to Luther, is the wonderful exchange: our sins upon him and his righteousness upon us. And you can see what Luther is doing here. Luther is developing and expounding and elaborating the fall, which Paul first spelled out at the end of 2 Corinthians 5:19–21. "In Christ God was reconciling the world to himself," says Paul. Question: How was he doing that? Answer: Next phrase, not imputing, not counting men's trespasses against them. God in Christ was reconciling the world to himself by not counting men's trespasses against them. How did God do that? How was God able to do that?

"For our sake, he [God the Father] made him [Jesus Christ, God the Son] to be sin who knew no sin, so that in him we might become the righteousness of God" (1 Cor. 5:21). Some commentators ex-

5 Luther, *Werke*, 48:12.

pound the phrase "made him to be sin" as meaning made him to be a sin offering. And that certainly is part of the truth. Grammatically, it's a perfectly possible view of the whole meaning of the phrase, but the flow of thought in the context makes me think that, in fact, it's not the whole meaning of the phrase. We have just heard that God in Christ reconciled the world to himself by not imputing men's trespasses to them. I conceive that Paul is here explaining how that was. When he says that the Father made the Son to be sin, him who knew no sin, that is him who was sinless in his own personal experience, what he's talking about is the Son of God being made sin by imputation of our sins to him. And I conceive that the flow of thought to the second half of the verse confirms that.

For Paul goes on to say, God did this "so that in him we might become the righteousness of God" (v. 21). And here, as several times in Paul's writings, he puts an abstract noun where you would have expected an adjective. He says, "we might become the righteousness of God," where you might have expected him to say, "we might become righteous before God." It seems to me that the natural way to read Paul's words is precisely in terms of the thought of the wonderful exchange that Luther has drawn out. God made him to be sin by imputing our sins to him, that in him, in union with him, we might become the righteousness of God—that is, might become righteous in God's sight through righteousness being imputed, reckoned to us.

Folly or Frenzy or Whatsoever

In other words, I read these words, just as Luther did. And just as Richard Hooker, that classical Anglican divine did, when at the end of his learned sermon on justification, he declared, in a wonderful sentence, "Let men count it folly or frenzy or whatsoever. . . . We care for no wisdom, no knowledge in the world, but this, that man has sinned and God has suffered; that God has made himself the sin of men, and that men are made the righteousness of God."[6]

This I conceive, is what Paul meant when he spoke of Christ crucified. This is how Paul understood the mediation of the Lord Jesus, that ministry which he fulfilled as the middleman, standing between God, the righteous Judge, and man, the ruined sinner, and bringing the two together, taking out of the way the obstacles that kept them apart.

Those obstacles are the guilt of our sins. And he took it out of the way. And so, reconciliation was accomplished, and God and man were brought together. I read my New Testament, and I find that the cross is its centerpiece, first to last. I find that in the declaration of Paul in Galatians 6:14, "But far be it from me to boast except in the cross of our Lord Jesus Christ."

Categories of the Cross

Jesus Christ is, in fact, an expression of the temper of the whole New Testament. For explaining the cross, the New Testament uses many images, many categories, many modes of thought blended together. These various categories and modes of thought serve to enrich our understanding of the cross and its meaning.

Sacrifice

The cross is represented for instance as sacrifice, as we're going to see more fully in a moment, whenever we hear of the blood

6 Richard Hooker, "Sermon on Habakkuk 1:4," (1585), in *The Works of Richard Hooker*, ed. John Keble, 5th ed. (Oxford, Oxford University Press, 1865), 3:490–91.

of Christ. In speaking of the blood of his cross, sacrificial ideas are being invoked.

Ransom

Similarly, the cross is represented as a ransom, not only a sacrifice for sins, but a purchase delivering us from captivity and jeopardy as the payment of a ransom does. Again, the cross is represented in the New Testament as victory, triumph over the devil and demonic forces. "Through death he might destroy the one who has the power of death, that is, the devil"—Christ broke his power—in order to "deliver all those who through fear of death were subject to lifelong slavery" (Heb. 2:14–15).

Colossians 2:15 agrees: "He disarmed the rulers and authorities and put them to open shame, by triumphing over them in him." To the eye of faith, at least, it's plain that Christ on the cross triumphed over demonic hosts and led them in his train as their conqueror. Whatever the world sees when it looks at the cross, that is what the eye of faith sees. Christ sloughed off the forces of evil, triumphing over them on the cross. There's the thought of victory.

Redemption

Again, the cross of Christ is represented in the New Testament in terms of redemption, a price paid for the freedom of a slave. We've already noted Paul using the category of reconciliation, the word that speaks of the mending of our broken relationship and the establishing of peace where previously there was alienation.

Propitiation

There is also in the New Testament that term *propitiation*, which the Revised Standard Version translates *expiation*, presumably under the influence of professor C. H. Dodd, who argued very influentially from 1930 onward that this word *hilastērion* in the Greek (and *hilasmós*) signifies only the putting away of sin from God's sight, but not the quenching of his wrath, because, said Professor Dodd, there is no personal wrath of God against sinners to be reckoned with. Suffice it to say that I believe Professor Dodd misconstrued the New Testament at that point.

And I take propitiation in the sense that, really, belief in the wrath of God compels one to take. Propitiation, according to the background of usage in secular Greek, and also in the Greek Old Testament, signifies the putting away of the wrath of God by removal of that which evokes it. And that I believe is precisely what it means to say, that the cross of Christ was a propitiation for our sins. That which provoked God's personal judicial hostility to us sinners was put away, namely the guilt of our sin.

Propitiation is a word expressing the complex idea of the quenching of God's wrath by the removal of that which evokes it, namely by the putting away of our sins. This is part of the glory of the cross. In all these terms, the cross is presented to us by these New Testament writers. And reading these passages as I do, I find myself constrained to affirm what the mainstream of Protestant theology has affirmed for centuries and more, namely, that the basic notion—the fundamental notion underlying all the other notions that concern the achievement of the cross—is the notion of substitution.

Substitution

The Son of God, who for us and for our salvation had become man, endured the sentence that a holy God had declared against our sins, in order that the guilty—you and I, the offenders—might go free, our sins being forgiven and our relationship with God being put right, which is what that phrase "righteous before God" or "the righteousness of God" means.

I don't find myself able to doubt that the notion of penal substitution (or penal satisfaction, as it used to be expressed) is in fact the heart of the New Testament message of the cross.

Satisfaction

Let me say a word about that term *satisfaction.* It's a word that has been used in Christian atonement theology from very early days. It first came into theology from Roman law. It signified that which is done in order to cancel out a legal obligation. Anselm, one of the pioneer Christian theologians of the atonement in the eleventh century AD, construed the notion of Christ's death as a satisfaction for sin in terms of what nowadays we would call damages, compensation—an offering made to God to satisfy his honor, his dignity, which our sins had outraged. Luther, more scripturally, expounded satisfaction in terms not of compensation for sin, but rather in terms of penal substitution, Christ passing under judgment for our sins. This is exactly what the New Testament is talking about.

This is also what our prayer book is talking about. When in the 1662 communion service, it instructs us to pray, it teaches us to give thanks to God for his tender love toward mankind, which prompted him to give his Son, who "made there, by his one oblation of himself once offered, a full, perfect, and sufficient sacrifice, oblation, and satisfaction" for our sins.

It's the same language as the Heidelberg Catechism had used at the end of the sixteenth century, when it taught the Christian to declare: "My only comfort in life and death is that I belong unto my faithful Savior, Jesus Christ, who with his precious blood has fully satisfied for all my sins."

Satisfaction is the old word, and I conceive it was a good one. It expresses the thought that Christ did all that needed to be done in order that our sins might be put away from God's sight.

Is Penal Satisfaction Biblical?

Very many in our day have challenged the scripturalness of this understanding of things and urged, by the aid of exegesis, as well as more general theological reasoning, that in saying these things, we are misinterpreting the New Testament witness. Therefore, I want to devote the thrust of this chapter to vindicating the account of the matter that I've just given you against its critics. Is this view, penal substitution—as I've called it, penal satisfaction, the old name—is this view scriptural, or is it not? That's the question.

Let me introduce my response to the suspicion that it isn't scriptural like this: As one reads Paul, who is the most elaborate expositor of the atonement in the New Testament, one discerns a certain hierarchy of concepts. He sees the cross, the crucifixion of Jesus Christ in which he glories, as achieving *redemption*—that is, deliverance from evil, deliverance from bondage—because it achieves *justification*, bringing forgiveness and a righteous standing with God. It achieves justification because it achieves *reconciliation*. It makes peace between ourselves and God. It achieves reconciliation by being an act of *propitiation*, quenching God's wrath by putting away sins. And it achieves propitiation just as it achieves redemption and reconciliation and justification, by being an act of blood-shedding—that is an act of *sacrifice*.

Paul speaks of our having redemption through Jesus's blood in Ephesians 1:7. He speaks of our being "justified by his blood" in Romans 5:9. He speaks of Christ's having reconciled us to God and made "peace by the blood of his cross" in Colossians 1:20. He speaks of God as having set the Savior forth "as a propitiation by his blood" in Romans 3:25. That word *blood*, as we've already said, points to sacrifice, points to those Old Testament rituals in which the blood of animals was shed for the sins of men. What, we ask, was the meaning of the shedding of blood in sacrifice?

Penal Substitution in the Old Testament

This has been much discussed in our day. It was fashionable at the beginning of the century to affirm that the meaning of the shedding of blood was not, as Bible students used to think, that hereby life was laid down in death by way of substitutionary offering. But rather, that hereby a life force, some kind of *mana*, some kind of energy, was released from the animal in whom it had resided, released for the reinvigorating of the relationship between men and God that sin had weakened and obstructed. That notion is going out of fashion now, partly as a result of the very brilliant work by Leon Morris,[7] but really, it's hard to read the Bible sympathetically and not feel, not indeed be constrained to judge, that the meaning of the shedding of blood is most certainly that hereby life is laid down in death as a substitutionary offering to atone for sin.

In Leviticus 17:11, we find God saying through Moses, concerning the sacrificial rituals of the Old Testament, "the life of the flesh is in the blood, and I have given it for you on the altar

7 See now Leon Morris, chapter 2, "Sacrifice," in *The Atonement: Its Meaning and Significance* (Downers Grove, IL / Leicester, England: Inter-Varsity Press, 1984).

to make atonement for your souls, for it is the blood that makes atonement by the life."

That could be taken as signifying that the blood makes atonement by reason of the release of vital energy to restore the relationship, though I don't think that that's a natural view, nor was it suggested by the context. But it becomes an extremely unnatural view, I think, when one links this Leviticus passage up with something in Numbers 35:31–34. Here God, through Moses, is laying down rules about the cities of refuge. God says,

> You shall accept no ransom for the life of a murderer, who is guilty of death, but he shall be put to death. And you shall accept no ransom for him who has fled to his city of refuge, that he may return to dwell in the land before the death of the high priest. You shall not pollute the land in which you live for blood [bloodshed, he means] pollutes the land, and no atonement can be made for the land for the blood that is shed in it, except by the blood of the one who shed it.

Pollution is only done away—that which hinders communion between God and his people in the land—is only removed by the shedding of the blood of the murderer.

Unless indeed the murderer remains throughout the life of the high priest in his city of refuge, which is the exception that God made. Otherwise, the only way in which the pollution brought on the land by the shedding of blood in murder can be removed is by the shedding of the blood of the murderer.

That looks like retribution, doesn't it? That looks like the doing of justice by which God is satisfied. That doesn't take us at all into the world of thought in which life is released for the renewing or revitalizing of a relationship. No, pollution is removed. That is the sphere of thought in which Leviticus 17:11 also moves.

When one looks at the sacrificial rituals, this impression is strongly confirmed. Take the regular trespass offering. How was it made? By the worshiper drawing near, that's the phrase that's used, which refers to his coming to the sanctuary. Drawing near with a perfect victim, a faultless animal, he places his hand on the head of the animal and kills it there at the sanctuary. Then the priest drains out the blood and pours the blood on one of the altars in the sanctuary. The significance of that action, surely, is as a witness to God—as a token, a testimony, a demonstration—that life has been taken according to God's ordinance to atone and make satisfaction for the sin that was done.

Or, look at the ritual of the Day of Atonement of which the writer to the Hebrews in his ninth chapter makes so much. When we give our Sunday school addresses on the Day of Atonement, we always, for some reason, train in our spotlight on the scapegoat. Now, the sins of the people are confessed over one of the two animals that's taken, over the scapegoat. And then the scapegoat is driven outside the camp, bearing the sins of Israel, bearing the sins of the people away. Yes, but what we should remember is that what was done with a scapegoat was only part of the ritual. There were two goats, not just one. The second goat was killed in the sanctuary. And as the writer to the Hebrews reminds us, that was the one occasion when each year the high priest would go into the Most Holy Place. It was itself a divinely given illustration and exhibition for the people to see and to learn from of what was actually being accomplished by the death of the other goat.

It was the blood-shedding on the Day of Atonement which, according to God's ordinance, was the guarantee of his forgiveness of the people's sins during that past year. We know from New Testament theology that these sacrifices had their efficacy through the blood of Christ which was to be shed, but which covered sins committed before Christ came, just as it covers sins committed since Christ came.

But that's not the point on which I'm focusing now. The point on which I'm focusing is that God associated the forgiveness of sins with the shedding of blood, the pouring out of life in death. And so in that great prophetic passage in which the servant of God is pictured as being made an offering for sin, he's stricken, he's killed, he's put to death for the sins of God's people. Thus, says Isaiah 53:10, God fulfills his pleasure to make the servant's soul an offering for sin. What we are seeing here surely can only naturally be interpreted in terms of substitution.

Substitutionary Righteousness

When we read Paul, spelling out to us the meaning of the cross of Christ in salvation terms, surely all doubt has finally vanished. Look again at Galatians 3:13. What is the flow of thought in Paul's own sentence? "Christ redeemed us from the curse of the law." Question: How? Answer: Being made a curse for us. The participial phrase is answering the question how. It's explanatory of the method. It's affirming substitutionary suffering. We've looked at 2 Corinthians 5:21, God "made him to be sin who knew no sin, so that in him we might become the righteousness of God."

A sin offering? Yes, for sure. Because, as I've already urged, we are to understand from the flow of thought in the context that our sins had been imputed to the Son of God, and he died thus as our victim, the innocent suffering for the guilty. In Colossians 2:14, Paul explains the cross in these terms. Let me pick up in verse 13, where the sentence begins and then we will get the flow of thought: "And you, who were dead in your trespasses and the uncircumcision of your flesh, God made alive together with him, having forgiven us all our trespasses, by canceling the record of debt that stood against us with its legal demands. This he set aside, nailing it to the cross." The bond, which stood against us with its legal demands, is quite certainly the law of God, with its requirement of total righteousness. The law of God here is viewed as, so to speak, an IOU, a statement of what we owe God.

We have not rendered the righteousness that we were obliged to render. We have broken the law. We have transgressed. Consequently, the IOU becomes our death warrant. We come under the penal sanctions of the law because we've broken it. Then, says Paul, God canceled this bond and set it aside. How did he do that? By nailing it to Christ's cross.

Surely we are to understand this in terms of the detail that all the evangelists record, that as was usual to Roman execution, the accusation, that is the statement of the crime for which the person was being executed, was nailed up on the cross so that everyone might see what it was that this person was being executed for.

The Eye of Flesh and the Eye of Faith

We know that, with the eye of flesh, what those who stood by the cross saw nailed up on it—as the accusation against Jesus, the crime of which he'd been found guilty—was, "Jesus of Nazareth, the king of the Jews" (John 19:19). He claimed to be the king of the Jews. He was executed for that claim. That's what the eye of flesh was shown by the accusation that Pilate had nailed up.

But, says Paul, the eye of faith sees beyond this. The eye of faith sees, nailed to Christ's cross, indicating that for which he's being put to death, the whole tally of our disobediences, the whole sad story of the points at which we fail to keep God's law. It's the same story that Paul is telling.

It's the same point that he's making. Penal substitution is the phrase that we need. Penal substitution is what's being spoken about. Finally, link with these passages from Paul the words in Romans 3:25–26, where Paul, having told us in a very compressed and weighty passage that God put forward his own Son to be a propitiation by his blood, continues: "This was to show God's righteousness, because in his divine forbearance he had passed over former sins. It was to show his righteousness at the present time, so that he might be just and the justifier of the one who has faith in Jesus" (Rom. 3:25–26). Now these verses have been much fought over by the exegetes. I see these verses in the flow of thought in Romans and judge therefore that the only natural way to take them is this: God set forth Christ as a propitiation by his blood to show his righteousness.

Judicial Righteousness

What righteousness is this? It's the righteousness that Paul has been talking about in the previous chapter, the righteousness of God who is going to show his hand in righteous judgment. Romans 2:5 speaks of the day of wrath and demonstration of the righteous judgment of God. It's judicial righteousness that's in view here. God's judicial righteousness had a question mark against it, because in his divine forbearance, he had passed over former sins. What are they? They are the sins that he did in fact forgive under the Old Testament, when men offered the prescribed sacrifices. In the nature of the case, it's not plain that the blood of an animal can put away the sin of a man in equity in strict justice.

It appears that God forgave sins without an adequate compensation or without an adequate offering. So there's a question mark against God's justice. Is he really going to judge sin? Is he really the God whose nature it is to judge every sin as it deserves? Yes, says Paul. Now that we can look at the cross of Christ we can see that it is so. Christ died as the substitute for every sinner who has transgressed, and whose sins are now forgiven, and as a substitute for every sinner who will transgress and whose sins will be forgiven. It was to show at this present time, says Paul, that God himself is righteous in judging sin.

He does in fact inflict the full penalty, wherever sin has been committed, but not on the sinner—rather on the sinner's substitute. He himself is righteous in judging sin. At the same time, by the means of his judging sin, the particular way that he does it, that is to show that he also justifies him who has faith in Jesus. Just justification—justification that is pardon and acceptance, based upon the judgment of our sins in the person of another—is the message which Paul is teaching here. So likewise in Romans 3 and on through Romans 4 and 5. Thus I read Paul as he explains the meaning of the cross of Christ. And on these biblical grounds, I maintain that penal substitution is indeed the phrase that we need in order to express the truth about Christ's cross.

There are objections and there are problems and there are difficulties raised, and our argument is not yet done. We must look at some of these problems and we must make some further points in order to vindicate belief in penal substitution against the criticisms that are brought.

Implications of Penal Substitution

So let me now branch out what I've said into five further points, which from one standpoint are no more than spelling out of the implications of what I've said already. But from another standpoint, there are important specifications of what's being said in order to answer critics.

1. The Definition of Substitution

The first point to make is a verbal one—a pipe-opener, we might say: the prejudice against the word *substitution* is misplaced. We find ourselves confronted with a whole host of writers who tell us the word *substitution* does not fit. What one should say about the cross of Christ is that it was vicarious and representative, but not substitutionary.

I think it's sufficient to answer that point from the dictionary. I open my Oxford English Dictionary, and I find that *substitution* is defined as "the putting of one person or thing in the place of another." I find then that when I look up *representation*, it's defined as "the fact of standing for, or in place of some other thing or person, substitution of one thing or person for another." And I find that the word *vicarious* is defined as "that which takes or supplies the place of another thing or person, substituted instead of the proper thing or person." And on the basis of the Oxford English Dictionary, I say, here is a distinction without a difference. The words *representative* and *vicarious* mean *substitutionary*.

And we might just as well call a spade a spade and use this clear and basic word.

2. The Character of Substitution

Second, the sphere of substitution is judicial. I wish to argue against those who say, and some do, that: we could conceive of a substitution that was not penal in character, but we balk at the idea of substitution under divine judgment. To those folk, I want to say: you have to reckon with the sphere of divine judgment, as both Scripture and our own moral experience introduce us to it.

Penal substitution, as a notion, does that.[8] That indeed is its glory. Penal substitution is a phrase that echoes the Latin *poena*, meaning penalty, and refers to the penalty due to us from God the Judge for wrong done and failure to meet his claims. This we've said.

Now the divine judicial context is a moral context also. God judges according to what is true and right. His judgment is not arbitrary, and he judges things as they are, whereas human judicial systems are not always rooted in moral reality. The Bible treats the worlds of moral reality and of divine judgment as coinciding. Divine judgment means that retribution is entailed by our past upon our present and future existence. God himself is in charge of this process.

He ensures, because it is right that he should ensure, that the objective wrongness and guiltiness of what we've been is always there to touch what we are now and what we are going to be. In the words of Emil Brunner, "Guilt means that our past—that

8 The following section, through the four concerns, is adapted from a section in J. I. Packer, "What Did the Cross Achieve? The Logic of Penal Substitution. The Tyndale Biblical Theology Lecture, 1973," *Tyndale Bulletin* 25 (1974): 3–45.

which can never be made good—always constitutes one element in our present situation."[9]

Surely that is a matter of moral reality and of actual moral experience. Guilt from the past does stretch out its hand to touch and blight our experience in the present. When Lady Macbeth, walking and talking, sees blood on her hand and doesn't know how to clean or sweeten that hand, she's witnessing to the order of retribution, as all writers of tragedy and surely all reflective men—certainly all reflective men who believe in the judgment of God—have come to know it. Wrongdoing may be forgotten for a time. David forgot his sin over Bathsheba and Uriah, but sooner or later, it comes back to mind, as David's sin did under Nathan's ministry. And at once conscience begins to work and our attention is absorbed and our peace and our pleasure are gone. And something tells us that we ought to suffer for the thing that we've done. The old Divines urge, when joined with inklings of God's displeasure for what we've done, this sense of things is in truth the start of hell—hell on earth.

It's in this context, of the actual experience of guilt and conviction of sin, that the truth of penal substitution is introduced, in order to focus for us four insights about our situation. And this is the way that Paul is applying it in those contexts from which I've quoted. Let me summarize the insights in order, in human terms like this.

INSIGHT 1: CONCERNING GOD

Insight 1 concerns God. It is that the retributive principle to which our consciences testify when they condemn us is God's sanction and is indeed an expression of the holiness and justice and good-

9 Emil Brunner, *The Mediator: A Study of the Central Doctrine of the Christian Faith*, trans. Olive Wyon (London: Lutterworth Press, 1934), 443.

ness that his law reflects. Death, spiritual as well as physical—the loss of the life of God as well as the life of the body—is the rightful sentence that he's announced against us and now prepares to inflict upon us.

INSIGHT 2: CONCERNING OURSELVES

Insight number 2 concerns ourselves. It is that standing in this way, under sentence: we are helpless either to undo the past or to shake off sin in the present. Thus we have no way of averting what threatens.

INSIGHT 3: CONCERNING JESUS

Insight 3 concerns our Lord Jesus Christ. It is that he took our place under divine judgment and received in his own personal experience all the dimensions of the death that was our sentence, whatever these were. So laying the foundation for our part on immunity, Luther expounded Scripture in these terms: "Christ himself suffered the dread and horror of a distressed conscience that tasted eternal wrath. . . . It was not a game, or a joke, or play-acting when he said, 'Thou hast forsaken me,' for then he felt himself really forsaken in all things, even as a sinner is forsaken."[10] And we say, do we not:

> We may not know, we cannot tell
> What pains he had to bear;
> But we believe it was for us
> He hung and suffered there.[11]

10 Luther, *Werke*, 5:602, 605.

11 Cecil Francis Alexander, "There Is a Green Hill Far Away" (1848).

He received in his own personal experience all the dimensions of the death that was our sentence, whatever these were, and so laid the foundation for our pardon and immunity.

INSIGHT 4: CONCERNING GUILT

The fourth insight, which the notion of penal substitution introduces into our actual experience of guilt and the bad conscience, has to do with faith. It is this: faith is a matter of first and foremost looking outside and away from oneself to Christ and his cross as the sole ground of present forgiveness and future hope. Faith sees that God's demands remain what they were and that God's law of retribution, which our consciences declare to be right, has not ceased to operate in his world nor ever will.

In our case, the law has operated already, in as much as all our sins, past, present, and even future, have been covered by Calvary. So our conscience is pacified by the knowledge that our sins have already been judged and punished in the person and death of another. So Bunyan's pilgrim before the cross loses his burden. And Augustus Toplady can assure himself (and here I quote a stanza from one of Toplady's hymns),

> If thou hast my discharge procured,
> And freely in my room endured
> The whole of wrath divine;
> Payment God cannot twice demand,
> First at my bleeding Surety's hand,
> And then again at mine.[12]

12 Augustus Toplady, "From Whence This Fear and Unbelief," 1844.

Reasoning thus, faith grasps the reality of God's free gift of righteousness, the rightness with God that the righteous enjoy, and faith grasps along with this the justified man's obligation to live henceforth "unto him which died for them, and rose again" as Paul says in 2 Corinthians 5:15 (KJV).

This is the sphere of substitution, the penal sphere. This is what substitution means, in terms of the actual human problem of actual human guilt, because the problem of actual human guilt is at the very heart of the human predicament and at the very heart of human misery. I am bold to affirm, as my ancestors in the gospel also affirmed, that penal substitution is in very truth the heart of the gospel, for it speaks directly to the very heart of human need.

3. The Solidarity of Substitution

But here quickly now, is a third point. The context of substitution is solidarity. What we have here in this great transaction, whereby God in Christ saves us from our sins, is not a legal fiction, but rather a case of solidarity whereby Christ involves us in his righteousness through union with him, as truly as Adam involved us in his sinning, through our union with him and his with us. Penal substitution is grounded in this ontological solidarity.

It's one moment in the larger mystery of what Luther called "the wonderful exchange" and what Morna Hooker has more recently called "interchange in Christ."[13] Distinguish these four moments in the mystery. First, the incarnation, when the Son of God came into the human situation, becoming man. Second, the cross, where Christ for us as our representative substitute, bore all

13 Morna D. Hooker, "Interchange in Christ," *JTS* 22 (1971): 349–61.

that we deserved for our sin in the way of divine judgment. But now the third moment in the interchange comes when through faith and God's gift of the Spirit, we become the righteousness of God in union with Christ and in solidarity with him (this echoes the logic of Romans 6 and Colossians 2.)

We, in solidarity with him, die painlessly and invisibly because he died painfully and publicly for us in substitution on the cross. We are united with him in his death and united with him in his resurrection. And it's thus, not otherwise, that his righteousness becomes ours. The effect of his atoning death becomes our pardon and the ground of our acceptance with God. We become the righteousness of God, not apart from him, but in him, on the basis of solidarity.

4. The Source of Substitution

Fourth, the source of substitution is divine love. So often it has been argued by critics of this doctrine that it divides the Trinity by representing a kindly Son placating a fierce and hostile Father in order to make him love men, which he did not do before.

That's a travesty. And that is utterly contrary to the Scripture witness to this mystery, which again and again roots everything in the love of God as the originating source of the atonement of Christ. "God is love," says 1 John 4:8. He goes on to explain his meaning, not in the way that modern liberals sometimes explain the theme of divine love, in terms of God being too kindly disposed toward his creatures finally to judge or banish any of them from his presence, or finally to take any account from them of their sin at all, but rather John explains the meaning of the love of God like this: "In this is love, not that we have loved God but," in a situation where we didn't, "that he loved us and sent his Son to be the propitiation for our sins" (4:10). Love, to be sure, is that which sent the Lord Jesus Christ to the cross, but it was the Father's love just as it was his own.

The source of substitution is the love of the Father and the Son, and, we may surely add, the Spirit. The Father, the Son, and the Holy Spirit are together in the work of atonement, wrought on the cross.

5. The Fruit of Substitution

The final point is simply this: the fruit of substitution is the salvation that Paul describes in 1 Corinthians 1:23, where having declared that "we preach Christ crucified" and understand the gospel in these terms, he goes on to spell out his meaning by saying, God is the source of your life in Christ Jesus, whom God made to be our "wisdom from God, righteousness and sanctification and redemption" (1:30).

Wisdom in the sense of the one who makes us wise with that wisdom that leads us into salvation; *righteousness* in the sense of his being the one who renders us righteous in God's sight; *redemption* in the sense that he is the one in whom we have redemption; *sanctification* in the basic sense that he is the one who brings us into a covenant relationship with God—committed to God from the human side, but yes, yes, but more important, accepted by God from the divine side—in virtue of atonement made. That's the fundamental meaning of sanctification in Scripture.

5

No Other Name

The Uniqueness of Jesus Christ

FROM THE PHRASE, "no other name," you can see what passage of Scripture I had in mind when I put this lecture together. I had in mind the words of Peter in Acts 4:12, in his speech to the Jewish leaders, "There is salvation in no one else, for there is no other name under heaven given among men by which we must be saved."

And it is the uniqueness of Jesus Christ as Savior about which I speak. We began these lectures, by taking as a kind of motto, a phrase to hold them all together, four words from Paul in 1 Corinthians 1:23, "We preach Christ crucified." These words, when you look at them, invite reflection on three things, two of which in fact have already passed before us in the four lectures that we've had together up to this point. It invites us first, this phrase, to reflect on the truth to be told. These words, "Christ crucified," point to the message that was folly to the Gentiles and a stumbling block to the Jews. At the beginning of our course of lectures, we raised the questions: What do these words mean? What are they talking about? How are we to spell them out, if we would grasp Paul's thought when he uses them?

Theological Truth

The Purpose of the Cross

We've made three points. They relate first to a cosmic purpose, whereby God the Creator is renewing his world. They relate to much more than private events in the inner psychic life. They relate to the reshaping of this whole cosmos. The title "Christ" points to the person who is at the center of history and through whom blessing for the cosmos comes in.

When speaking of Christ crucified, Paul is setting what he has to say about Jesus in the context of this cosmic purpose of God, what he calls "the mystery of his will" in Ephesians 1:9, to head up, sum up, reintegrate all things in Christ. Indeed all things will be reintegrated in Christ, so Christians believe, when he comes again. That was the first point. "Christ crucified" is a phrase that fits into this cosmic, renewing purpose of God.

The Person of the Cross

Second, it's a phrase that points to deity in the person who went to the cross. If you ask Paul: Who was the Christ? Paul replies without hesitation: Jesus of Nazareth, the Son of God. This Christ, being God incarnate, is the Christ who is there. So, we said, the Christ who is here whenever his word is preached. He is the Son of God, who was the Father's agent in creating and sustaining the universe and has now become the Father's agent in redeeming it (Colossians 1).

This is that to which the word *crucified* points, for it was through the cross that the Son of God, who became by incarnation the man Jesus, redeemed the world. We made this point in opposition to those who affirm that the theology that declares Jesus to be divine is a deifying myth, telling us no more than the private and personal significance, the transforming impact, which the Spirit-filled man, Jesus of Nazareth, has upon those who come in contact with him.

The Event of the Cross

There's a third point to which the words refer. That word *crucified* points to the event of the cross. And we saw in our last study together how Paul expands the event of the cross as a substitutionary sacrifice for men's sins, a sacrifice that we needed if ever we were to find forgiveness and acceptance with God, an effective sacrifice that actually does bring righteousness, that is, a right relationship with God, to those who put their faith in the Christ who made it.

The Truth of the Cross

We began to raise at one point this question: Is all this that Paul was affirming true? And we began to develop a historical apologetic for an affirmative answer to that question. The historical facts appear to say, yes, it is true. It does appear that Jesus Christ was much more than a Spirit-filled man. It does appear that he rose from the dead. It is incredible that the New Testament should be as it is, or indeed that the Christian church should ever have started as the community of the resurrection, had he not done so. And this points away from the notion that he's a mere spirit-filled man and provides powerful evidence for the truth of Paul's declaration that he was divine. So these are the things that we've seen with regard to the truth that's to be told.

The Witnesses of the Cross

The second thing to which the words of Paul, "we preach Christ crucified" (1 Cor. 1:23) invite us to turn our minds is the tellers of this truth. "We preach," says Paul. One asks: Who is the "we"? It's clear that in the first instance, Paul is talking about himself and his fellow apostles, of whom he says in 2:6, "we speak," or "we do impart," wisdom to the mature, in a mystery that is in a revealed secret from God, something that God has now made known to us. And in verses 12 and 13 of 1 Corinthians 2, Paul is more specific about God's work of making it known to us—making it known, that is, to the apostles—for he writes, "We have received not the spirit of the world, but the Spirit who is from God that we might understand the things freely given us by God. And we impart this in words not taught by human wisdom but taught by the Spirit." There you have the characteristic apostolic claim to inspiration. Here is Paul claiming that the authority of apostolic teaching derives from the fact that it's God's own instruction shown to the apostles and then mediated through the apostles in words that the Holy Spirit teaches.

We noted that when one reads the New Testament, one finds that there is solidarity of testimony and convergence in witness. Despite all the different phrases and forms of speech that are used of Jesus of Nazareth, his divine person and his atoning work, the thrust of this many-stranded testimony is one.

We might here raise the question: Is it only the apostles then who are to tell this truth? We began at the end of our last study to see that, as fellow believers with them, it is for us to take our stand as fellow witnesses beside them, proclaiming the same truth that has had the same transforming power in our lives as it had in theirs.

The Preaching of the Cross

Now we come to the third matter on which these words invite us to reflect, the matter that is going to be our special concern in this lecture, namely, the task of telling. "We preach," says Paul. "We preach Christ crucified." Question: When and where? Paul's answer: All the time and everywhere. You remember Paul's phrase in Colossians 1:28, "Him we proclaim, warning everyone and teaching everyone with all wisdom."

As far as Paul is concerned, every man must know, and he makes it his life's work to see, as far as in him it lies, that every man does know. Why, we ask? And the Bible immediately comes up with this answer. There is a universal command to publish this good news. There is a universal claim, which Jesus Christ makes on all mankind. And there is a universal need, which all men share and which the gospel alone can meet. All these thoughts, I think, are implicit in the word *must*, when Peter says, "There is no other name under heaven given among men by which we *must* be saved" (Acts 4:12). The universal command, "Go . . . and make disciples," is there in Matthew 28:19. It's the Great Commission, and it's surely familiar to us all. "Go . . . make disciples of all nations," says our Lord. Similarly in Acts 1:8, he says to the apostles, "You will be my witnesses in Jerusalem and in all Judea and Samaria, and to the ends of the earth," and hereby he focuses the thought that this message is to go to the outermost parts of the earth. The reason why is made plain when later on in the Acts narrative, we find Paul at Athens declaring in Acts 17:30, God "commands all people everywhere to repent." This is a message for all the world and must go to all the world. This is a matter of divine command.

The Claim of the Cross

There is a universal claim made by the Christ of this gospel. The claim is that he is the one way, the only way, to the knowledge of God as Father. John 14:6 may here be quoted again. "I am the way, and the truth, and the life. No one comes to the Father except through me." This is news that all the world needs, for every man is claimed by Christ to enter into the knowledge of God the Father, and those who hear the gospel and decline so to enter will be judged for refusing life.

The Need for the Cross

This leads to the third thought, that there is a universal human need, inasmuch as there is no hope for any man or woman apart from the gospel of Christ crucified. Only Jesus Christ brings hope into fallen human lives.

You remember how, in the letter to the Romans, Paul analyzes out the state of fallen man under law, under sin, under God's wrath, the threat of his judgment for our transgressions, and under death here and now in the present. Death reigns over all those who are found in Adam. This is where man is, and this determines his destiny if he's out of Christ. He sums up his testimony in Ephesians 2:12, where he reminds the believers that when they were separated from Christ, they were without God, and without hope in the world. If this is the state of men and the prospect for men without Christ, then it's plain that compassion must be a motive in the communicating of the gospel. We take the word to the world, not only out of obedience to Christ, in order that his claim on men may be made known, but out of compassion to our fellow human beings who need this message so desperately. It's a matter of obeying the first commandment, loving our Lord, and of obeying the second commandment, loving our neighbor. It's both those things together when the gospel is proclaimed.

Evangelicals have always understood the matter in this way. They have seen the call to spread the gospel, as a matter both of obedience to the Lord's command and of compassionate service to our fellow men and women. And so, ever since the eighteenth century, they have given themselves to spread the gospel through the world, seeking thereby the world's salvation. One thinks of William Carey making much of the Great Commission to go and make disciples of all the nations, insisting that this was a summons to the whole Christian church and not simply to the apostles, and giving the church that tremendous motto: "Expect great things of God; attempt great things for God."[1]

One thinks of John Mott in the last century, bringing into being the student volunteer movement, with its motto *The Evangelization of the World in This Generation*, to "evangelize to a finish and bring back the king." And in more recent days, one thinks of the Berlin and Lausanne Congresses avowedly on world evangelization.

1 William Carey, "The Deathless Sermon" (May 30, 1792), Friar Lane Baptist Church, Nottingham, England.

For two hundred years now, this has been a central concern of evangelical people, the world over: spreading the gospel throughout the length and breadth of the earth. But in the second half of this twentieth century, the obstacles to winning the world to faith in Christ seemed to have increased. The world's population is exploding. It's now well over 4 billion and rapidly increasing. Though by absolute standards, the number of Christians in the world is increasing (never mind what is happening in countries like England and Australia). Also the fact remains that Christians are a shrinking minority proportionately in this world, in which the population explodes so fast. Proportionately, there is a smaller percentage of Christians in the world's population than there was before.

Furthermore, doors are closing—closing in some cases with a resounding clash. Something like one third of the world's population dwells behind the iron curtain, under circumstances in which the preaching of the gospel is either very difficult or impossible because of the degree of opposition that the government makes to that activity.

Furthermore, this is the age in which the ethnic religions—Hinduism and Buddhism in the East, and let's for our purposes bracket with them Islam, which though from one standpoint, it's an offshoot of Christianity, is nonetheless ethnic, in a very obvious sense—are gaining ground, reviving the sense of their own strength, dignity, and potential, and invading the West, seeking to make converts.

If one judges by the numerical figures it does not look as if the gospel is really making headway in the world, looking at the whole situation in overall global terms. In this situation, one cannot wonder if some, at least, find their nerve failing them. And their minds move to speculations and theories, which explore the possibility that the conviction, that all have need to hear the gospel, the certainty that Christians are debtors to all the world to share the gospel with all men, ought perhaps to be modified. "Is it really so?" men have asked. Have we not perhaps overplayed our hand in the past in assuming it was so?

Theological Speculations

What I want to do is to glance at three such speculations, none of which seem to me to be acceptable. I'll declare that right at the outset.

First, the speculation that there is divine saving power in all religions. That's a speculation embraced by liberal and radical Protestants very freely. The speculation, secondly, that within the non-Christian religions of the world, you find what we may call "anonymous Christianity." That's a Roman Catholic equivalent of speculation number 1. And the third speculation is dogmatic universalism, the belief that God will finally bring to glory every rational spirit whom he has made. Let's look at these speculations in order and see what can be said for them.

Pluralism: All Religions Save

First, the speculation that there is divine saving efficacy in all religions. Whence one asks, does this idea come? The answer: in the Protestant world at any rate, it is based on Friedrich Schleiermacher's view. Schleiermacher was the grandfather of liberalism, a distinguished theologian of the early years of the nineteenth century. He taught that the essence of religion is the same wherever you find it, that religion is a sense of dependence on the divine, and that this sense is the common core of all religions. So the only difference between one religion and another is the degree of purity with which this sense of dependence on the divine is articulated in words.

Followers of Schleiermacher in this century have been the German Ernst Troeltsch, the American William Ernest Hocking, the German Paul Tillich, the Englishman Arnold Toynbee, and the Englishman John Hick, all of whom have argued in their own way that Schleiermacher's view is indeed correct. And God is doing essentially the same thing for men through all the religions that the world knows. Here, for instance, are some words expressing the position in dogmatic form:

> Christianity is a way of salvation, which beginning some 2,000 years ago has become the principal way of salvation in three continents. The other great world faiths are likewise ways of salvation, providing the principal path to the divine reality for other large sections of humanity.[2]

The view of missions, to which this belief leads, is that it is proper for representatives of one religion to go and cross-fertilize other faiths with their own insights. By so doing, they will not displace those other faiths. All they will do is enrich them. It's in these terms that the missionary task should be conceived. It's rather like a situation in which, from different parts of the world, there are any number of airlines that will fly you to New York. It doesn't really matter on which of the airlines you travel. You'll get to New York, whichever one it is. The food served, the dress worn by the hostesses, the languages spoken on the planes will vary, but New York is the destination in every case.

2 John Hick, *God and the Universe of Faiths: Essays in the Philosophy of Religion* (London: Macmillan, 1973).

Or, you can put it in the way that our theosophy friends love to do. We are all climbing the same mountain, all adherents of the different faiths that the world knows. And we shall all meet at the top. So was Jesus unique? Only in degree, at most: only in the vividness with which he showed men the way of openness to God, total commitment to the lure and the pressure of the divine, and selfless living for the welfare of others as one follows the lure of the divine.

This is part of the view of Christianity put forward in the book, *The Myth of God Incarnate*, to which I've made reference before. I think perhaps in fairness, I had better quote directly from the book, for I don't want you to think that I'm in any way guiling it. I'm reading, therefore, the words of John Hick about Jesus:

> I see the Nazarene as intensely and overwhelmingly conscious of the reality of God. He was a man of God living in the unseen presence of God and addressing God as Abba Father. His spirit was open to God, and his life a continuous response to the divine love as both utterly gracious and utterly demanding. He was so powerfully God-conscious that his life vibrated as it were to the divine life. And as a result, his hands could heal the sick and the poor in spirits were kindled to new life in his presence. If you or I had met him in first century Palestine, we would, we may hope, have felt deeply disturbed and challenged by his presence. We would have felt the absolute claim of God confronting us, summoning us to give ourselves wholly to him and to be born again.[3]

3 John Hick, "Jesus and the World Religions," *The Myth of God Incarnate*, ed. John Hick (London: SCM Press, 1977), 172.

That, of course, in John Hick is just metaphor. It's a metaphor for a new start. "And to be born again as his children and as agents of his purposes on earth." And so on.

Schleiermacher himself could not have put it better. That is a pure statement, in 1977 terms, of the Schleiermacher position. If now we ask what John Hick thinks about other religions, well, in the same essay he has told us quite explicitly. Again, for fairness, let me read his words:

> All salvation—that is, all creating of human animals into children of God—is the work of God. The different religions have their different names for God acting savingly towards mankind. Christianity has several overlapping names for this—the eternal Logos, the cosmic Christ, the second person of the Trinity, God the Son, God the Spirit. If, selecting from our Christian language, we call God-acting-towards-mankind the Logos [the Word], then we must say that all salvation, within all religions, is the work of the Logos and that under their various images and symbols men in different cultures and faiths may encounter the Logos and find salvation. But what we cannot say is that all who are saved are saved solely and exclusively by Jesus of Nazareth.[4]

Well, again, this is a pure statement of the position. All religions have saving significance for those who adhere to them, says Hick. It is just an accident of geography that we who were born in the lands where Christianity is dominant have been brought up on Christianity. No more is given to us through Christianity than is

4 John Hick, *God Has Many Names* (Louisville, KY: Westminster John Knox, 1982), 175.

given to the Hindu through his Hinduism or the Muslim through the worship of Allah. This is the view.

What are we to say of it? One has to say quite forcefully that it's utterly out of touch with the Bible's view of Christian religion, which is summed up for us in a passage like 1 Thessalonians 1:9 and following, in which Paul says that the Thessalonian converts turned from idols to serve a living and true God and to wait for his Son from heaven. Or, by a passage like Romans 1:18 and following, where the religions of the pagan world are interpreted by the apostle, as in truth, so many expressions of apostasy from God, the Creator. Romans 1:18–23 spells this idea out in very clear detail, and Emil Brunner's way of paraphrasing what Paul is there saying seems to me to be a very fair statement of the apostle's thrust:

> The God of the "other religions" is always an idol. The religious forms of the imagination always follow the law of secularization, either in the form of making finite-idolatry in the ordinary polytheistic sense—or in the form of depersonalization, in which the idea of God is involved into an abstraction [God ceases to be a person and becomes a principle]. . . . If the secularization, the blending of God with nature and man, is the first phenomenon, then the *cor incurvatum in se*, [he's quoting Augustine here: "the heart bent back on itself"] egocentricity, or anthropocentrism, or eudaemonism, that is, the failure to give glory to God, or self-seeking, is the deepest motive of all the "other religions." . . . The original sin of man breaks out first of all, and mainly, in his religion: the essence of original sin is man's apostasy and his inveterate tendency to be absorbed in himself.[5]

5 Emil Brunner, *Revelation and Reason: The Christian Doctrine of Faith and Knowledge* (Philadelphia, PA, 1946), 264.

This seems to me to be a true summary of what Paul is saying in Romans 1:18 and following, as he diagnoses the case of mankind, holding down God's truth in unrighteousness, refusing to worship his Creator and instead worshiping the creature.

If one looks now at the works of other religions, it seems hard to exclude them from the condemnation, which is implicit in our Lord's own words in the Sermon on the Mount, about the pagans who use vain repetitions in prayer, thinking that they will be heard for their much speaking. The prayer of the ethnic religions, and with it the religious practice, is entirely a matter of doing things to commend oneself to God.

This has been demonstrated over and over, and it remains true despite the well-meant efforts of a theologian like Raimon Panikkar, who in his book, *The Unknown Christ of Hinduism* (1964), argues that the morality and the good life of the Hindu corresponds to the saving sacraments of Christianity. One has to say, this is really something very different from the life of grace which Christians know. This is the religion of works, as distinct from the religion of grace. It's not in the least plausible to suggest that here you have the same essence of religion as you have in Christianity. More might be said, but I must move on.

Roman Catholicism: Anonymous Christians Will Be Saved

I want now to look at the Roman Catholic speculation, which corresponds to this, the notion namely of "anonymous Christianity," as it is called by its leading exponent Karl Rahner. What we're looking at here is the development historically of the Roman Catholic exposition of the formula, "outside the church there is no salvation." Roman Catholic thinking, as you know, starts from the belief that there is no other church save the communion that acknowledges the Bishop of Rome as its head. "Protestant ecclesial communities," as the second Vatican council called them, are not strictly the church, although they exhibit certain features of the church. As for pagans, there is no question of their being in the church, at least outwardly. And from the third century onward for many centuries, the characteristic exposition of the proposition "outside the church there's no salvation" was that salvation comes through sharing directly in the sacramental life of the one fold. And without this, there is no hope for anyone.[6]

This view pertained in that simple form until the sixteenth century, when the Council of Trent opened the door an inch to the pagans, or at least to the unbaptized, by teaching that baptism could be received not only *in re* (that is, in physical reality, through the actual application of water in a baptismal service), but also *in voto* (that is, in purpose or vow or resolve). For this, the name given was "baptism of desire," and it was held to be a reality before God where circumstances made water baptism impossible.

An example would be the case of the thief on the cross who put faith in Jesus, but for whom no question of water baptism could arise. So Trent taught that anyone who in his heart desired baptism, but wasn't able to have it, was counted in among the saved, even though the saving sacrament of baptism had never become a reality for his experience.

And then in 1863, in an encyclical, Pius IX opened the door a little further by affirming of pagans, Protestants, and Eastern

6 The following twelve paragraphs are adapted from J. I. Packer, "The Way of Salvation, Part IV: Are Non-Christian Faiths Ways of Salvation?" *BSac* 130:518 (April 1973): 111–14.

Christians that "those who labor under ignorance of the true religion, if this ignorance is invincible, are not held guilty in this respect in the Lord's eyes."[7] In other words, they will not be held guilty whose ignorance is dominant and incurable, not because of negligence or ill will or any intention of disobeying God, but wholly owing to conditioning of such a sort as to make it impossible for them to recognize the true religion.

Link this with what Trent said and the possibility at once emerges that a person may in good faith, through "invincible ignorance," reject at a conscious level the true church—of course, in terms of the theory, the Roman Church is the true church—believing it to be false and idolatrous as Protestants did and many do. And at the same time, they may unconsciously belong to it by desire—*in voto*, you see. They want to be in the true church, but they can't recognize the Roman Church is the true church.

This is the line that Roman Catholics from that time onward have pursued in order to explain how non-Roman Catholics can be saved. When in 1949, a certain Father Leonard Feeney of Boston taught that all non-Roman Catholics are doomed to damnation, the Holy Office in Rome sent Archbishop Richard Cushing a letter condemning this teaching as heretical, and excommunicating any who held it. And that was the end of Father Feeney's public ministry.[8]

7 Henrici Denzinger, ed., *Enchiridion Symbolorum*, 30th ed. (Friburg, 1955), 1647.

8 The facts are reported by Hans Küng, "The Freedom of Religions," *Attitudes toward Other Religions*, ed. Owen C. Thomas (London, 1969), 201. The proposition "outside the Church there is no grace," maintained by the Jansenists, had been condemned long before (Denzinger, *Enchiridion Symbolorum*, 1379).

In 1964, the Second Vatican Council went yet further along this line:

> But if some men do not know the Father of our Lord Jesus Christ, yet acknowledge the Creator, or seek the unknown God in shadows or images, then God himself is not far from such men. . . . Those who, while guiltlessly ignorant of Christ's gospel and of his Church, sincerely seek God and are brought by the influence of grace to perform his will as known by the dictates of conscience, can achieve eternal salvation. Nor does divine providence deny the assistance necessary to salvation to those who, without having attained, through no fault of their own, to an explicit knowledge of God, are striving, not without divine grace, to lead a good life.[9]

It is of course, characteristic of Roman Catholic theology to believe that grace permeates all the life of all men and that the fallen human heart, despite the weakness that sin has brought upon it, has not become utterly anti-God in its inclinations. On this basis, it's comparatively easy for Roman Catholics to say, "Well, everyone deep down is striving godward, and God, seeing this, acknowledges it." This very striving is counted as implicit faith and becomes the means of their salvation. That really seems to be what is being said.

Three years prior to Vatican II, the distinguished Roman Catholic divine, Karl Rahner, had put forward the following line of argument. This is a yet fuller statement of what's implicit in the Vatican statement and was implicit in what had gone before: The

9 "Dogmatic Constitution on the Church," ii.16, in *The Documents of Vatican II*, ed. Walter M. Abbott, trans. Joseph Gallagher (London, 1966), 35.

exclusive claims of Christianity operate only where Christianity is known; non-Christian faiths, which are the combined products of grace and sin, function as "legitimate" and saving religions wherever Christianity is absent; their adherents should therefore be classed as "anonymous Christians" having "implicit faith" (that is, a disposition to believe what the Church believes); and the Church's missionary task is to make explicitly Christian the faith of the anonymously Christian world, as Paul did at Athens, by introducing the God who was already being worshiped, though in ignorance (Acts 17:23).[10] Much thinking along this line, positing a vast saving work of God outside the church's fold, appears in modern Roman Catholic theology. This is the kind of speculation that underlies the statement of Vatican II and is treated therefore by Roman Catholics, at least in the majority of cases, as being almost axiomatically true. What are we to make of this idea? It seems to me that the following things have to be said.

First, Rahner's idea is speculation and has a thrust quite different from that of Paul's Athenian speech, which condemned idolatry without in any way justifying idolatry.

Second, it's a stubborn fact that non-Christian religions are radically different from Christianity. On Rahner's view, one would expect to find some fundamental correspondence or convergence, but Owen Thomas does seem to be correct when he writes:

> The modern study of religions has made it extremely difficult, if not impossible, to demonstrate that an ideal essence lies at the heart of all of them. . . . The so-called higher religions do not

10 Karl Rahner, "Christianity and the Non-Christian Religions," *Theological Investigations*, trans. Karl H. Kruger (London, 1966), 5:115–35.

> stand closer together than the earlier or lower forms, but are in fact more sharply divided from each other. . . . The adherence of the other religions honestly cannot see their deepest intuitions fulfilled in Christianity. If you have ever talked to an erudite Muslim, Buddhist, or Hindu, you will know how true that is. There are in fact decisive differences among the religions in regard to the nature of the divine and of human fulfillment.[11]

What he is saying is that the facts do not fit the theory. It really does appear that the world religions are going off in a different direction from that in which Christianity goes.

Third, if non-Christian faiths are ways of salvation till Christianity comes, but not after, then as Owen Thomas pointedly observes, "It might be safer for the adherence of the other religions if the Christian message were kept a secret."[12] Quite so! The Christian mission would then be less a service than a disservice to the world. The missionary would have to choose between either the dishonesty of concealing or the lunacy of admitting that the first effect of his bringing the gospel is to destroy a possibility of salvation that was there before. Now surely this is a *reductio ad absurdum* of Rahner's whole idea.

And then over and above all that, as we saw a moment ago, Rahner's speculation disregards, and in fact contradicts, the biblical view of non-Christian faiths as being rooted in apostasy and as being therefore manifestations of human religiosity, which are essentially guilty rather than good.

11 Owen C. Thomas, "Introduction," in *Attitudes toward Other Religions*, ed. Owen C. Thomas (London, 1969), 22–23.

12 Thomas, "Introduction," 24.

I find myself then unable to go along with either the Protestant or the Roman Catholic form of the speculation that there is real saving religion—religion that is essentially of the same character as Christian faith—outside the sphere in which faith in Christ exists.

I will concede (and this of course is no new point, others have made it before me) that if God should, by some kind of special direct revelation, bring persons who have never heard of Christianity to acknowledge their sin, according to the light of conscience, and heartily repent of it and trust him for its forgiveness, then indeed it would be forgiven and those folk would be saved by grace, and in a life beyond this, even if not here, they would find that they had been saved by Jesus Christ. That I readily concede. What I do not know is whether this ever happens. And in the absence of any such knowledge, I find myself going along still with what Peter said, in the words with which this lecture began, "There is no other name under heaven given among men whereby we must be saved" (Acts 4:12).

Universalism: All Will Be Saved

Thirdly, I want to glance for a moment at universalism, a very widespread and popular theory these days; a theory that is put forward as an optimism, not of nature, as if no man were bad enough for God to condemn, but of grace, the supposition being that part of the triumph and victory of Christ on the cross was that his death guaranteed the salvation of all men that ever have been or ever will be. It sounds extremely honoring to the Father and the Son to make such a suggestion. It certainly fits in with what I would like to believe, and you too I am sure. For I would think there was something wrong with you if you told me that you really would not like to be able to believe that all men everywhere will finally be saved. It would be very comfortable doctrine. It would take away from life one of the things, one of the awarenesses, that makes all life uncomfortable to a degree for Christian people.

But the question is, will the Bible allow us to be universalists? The universalist thesis, at least as expounded among Protestants, takes this form: That all the threats that the New Testament pronounces against those who reject the word of Christ are true, and folk will enter into hell. And that is to say they will enter into an experience of the kind into which the rich man in our Lord's parable entered, an experience of pain and distress for their ungodliness on earth. But this will not be their final state. The universalist speculation is that hell will be ultimately untenanted.

Hell, thus, does for unbelievers on this theory what purgatory does for believers on Roman theory. That is, it makes them fit for heaven. Universalism appears as a doctrine of salvation out of what the New Testament calls eternal destruction, eternal punishment, perdition, and so on.

The thought is that in that state, men will have a further encounter with Jesus Christ and his offer of mercy. For some, it will be a second chance, for others who never heard the gospel, it will be their first chance. The universalists are confident that this encounter will issue in a positive response, leading to the transition from the state of chastening distress for sin into the state of final joy and glory. Thus, all men finally will be saved.

To focus this, do realize that universalism is the doctrine of the salvation even of Judas. This theory ought to be tested out with reference to the case of Judas about which we know a good deal from the New Testament.

Time doesn't allow us to go into all the details of the arguments that universalists put forward for their view. From the way that I've expounded it, you have perhaps already come to think yourselves that it's a somewhat hazardous view to argue on the basis of Holy Scripture. It doesn't sound in the least like anything that the Bible says.

One remembers how, for instance, in our Lord's parable—if parable is the right name for it—is a story of what will be the destiny for the sheep and for the goats. The story ends with the one class of folk going away into eternal life (*zoe aionios*), and the other class of folk going away into eternal punishment (*kolasis aionios*) (Matt. 25:46). And the word *aionios* in both cases signifies that which belongs to the age to come—the last stage, the final age, the final state. And therefore it implies endlessness, it would appear, in both instances.

There are no compelling arguments from Scripture that the universalists can bring where they can quote texts, which taken in isolation seem to point in this direction of everyone being finally saved. The same authors from which those texts are quoted make other statements elsewhere, which shows that they at least did not expect universal salvation in this way.

Just one example of many: from the fourth Gospel, from the words of our Lord himself, it is true that he said, "I, when I am lifted up from the earth, will draw all people to myself" (John 12:32). But it's also true that he said, and indeed he had earlier said, "An hour is coming when all who are in the tombs will hear his voice and come out, those who have done good to the resurrection of life, and those who have done evil to the resurrection of judgment" (John 5:28–29)—which does not sound like universal salvation. There are many more examples of this that could be given.

When theological arguments are offered as a basis for inferring universal salvation, they run up against obstacles and the biblical testimony. The statement that "God is love," in 1 John 4:8, is preceded by the statement that "God is light" (1 John 1:5).

And when John Robinson, for instance, argues that the divine justice is a function of the divine love, that does not seem to square with what 1 John is saying. Again, we have to face the fact that the New Testament insists that there's no salvation where there's no faith, and gives us no answer to the question: How, if God's presentation of his love and his gospel to men, doesn't move them in this life, we are entitled to assume that it is bound to move them in a life to come?

A quotation, which goes the rounds, I don't know where it originated, is this: "No soul is lost until God has thrown his arms about it in eternity and looked long into its eyes." One can see there what is being said. But the question has to be: Could the Lord Jesus in any future life do more to exhibit love to Judas, and look longer and more effectively into the eyes of Judas, than he did in this world? And if Judas was impervious to all that in this world, is there any good reason to suppose that Judas's heart will be any different in the world to come?

I don't pursue the argument further. What I'm concerned to show by reasoning in this way is that the whole position is speculative. And what I want to say now, in rounding off my all-too-brief review of universalism, is that there seem to be three biblical counterarguments, which so far from being speculative, are biblically inescapable, which in my judgment, make it quite impossible to entertain the universalist view.

I will put these three counterarguments in the form of questions.

1. UNIVERSALISM AND MAN'S DECISIONS

Does not universalism ignore the biblical stress on the decisiveness of this life's decisions for the determining of destiny? Think again of Judas. Our Lord said of Judas, in Matthew 26:24, "The Son of Man goes as it is written of him, but woe to that man by whom the Son of Man is betrayed. It would have been better for that man if he had never been born." Do you think Jesus would have spoken so of a man to whose final salvation he looked forward?

There are many more Scriptures that point in the same direction. What, we may ask, is so terrible about Jesus's warning to the Jews in John 8:21–24, that if they don't believe that he is the one whom God has sent, they will die in their sin. If they are ultimately to be saved, is this a final disaster, and should it be spoken of as a final disaster?

Why did Jesus insert into the parable of the rich man and Lazarus the detail that between the one and the other, in that future state into which they passed, a great gulf was fixed so that no one could pass from either side to the other?

Well, there are many Scriptures that point in this direction and seem abundantly to warrant, what Baron von Hügel, the Roman Catholic lay theologian of the early years of this century, called the "affirmation of abiding consequences," the decisiveness of this life's decisions as determining what will be hereafter. Does not universalism ignore this? I think it does.

2. UNIVERSALISM AND GOSPEL PREACHING

A second point is the focusing of a dilemma that universalists, I think, cannot avoid. It is for them to choose on which horn of it they would prefer to be impaled. *Does not the universalist hypothesis condemn the preaching of Christ and the apostles as being either inept or immoral?* Either inept, because they were ignorant that all will be saved, and so talked as if all wouldn't be, or immoral, because they knew that all would be saved in the end—but concealed that fact in order to bluff people into the kingdom, by using the fear motive?

This is a painful dilemma to formulate, and you must excuse its uncouthness, but I want to put it sharply. The universalist must settle for one or other of those two alternatives. I leave it to him to choose which. But I myself reject the dilemma, for I reject the doctrine.

3. UNIVERSALISM AND CHRISTIAN CONSCIENCE

Here is my third consideration, which again I put in the form of a question: *Is not universalism rejected by each Christian's own conscience?* Here I quote a word from James Denney who said, "I dare not say to myself that if I forfeit the opportunity [that is, the spiritual opportunity] this life affords, I shall ever have another; and therefore I dare not say so to another man"[13]—nor dare I say so of another man. How could I? I know no answer to that.

13 James Denney, *Studies in Theology* (London, 1895), 244.

I find myself then concluding that we would be wise not to put our eggs in the universalist basket. It is an attractive speculation, but not a scriptural one. Scripture obliges us to live with the uncomfortable certainty that folk who are Christless, who live and die Christless, are, in some real substantial sense of the word, lost. Scripture requires us to make our life's policy on the basis that this is indeed so.

A Perishing World

Where are we left, then? What sort of life policy does Scripture require us to make? We are left with a world of which Paul himself says, more than once, that it is perishing. "The word of the cross is folly to those who are perishing," he says (1 Cor. 1:18). His word *perishing* is simply factual. This is the state. This is the way that they are. This is the measure of their need. The world is lost. "The whole world lies in the power of the evil one" (1 John 5:19). Men without Christ are indeed without hope, but we are left also with a sufficient Savior, Christ crucified. Christ, the power and wisdom of God, the risen, reigning Lord, who in the power of his atoning work and of his heavenly ministry is adequate to meet the needs of every human being and to support men in every situation into which he may enter.

This Savior brings us salvation, which we may say is man-size. It is our privilege to proclaim him and to declare that though "there is no other name given under heaven among men whereby we must be saved," through the name of Christ, all may be saved. He is the sufficient and adequate Savior and deliverer in all human need and extremity.

A Sovereign God

We are left further with a sovereign God, who though he owes salvation to none, is doing a saving work through the word in almighty grace to create to himself a people, a new humanity. The gospel calls us to identify with this new humanity as recipients of the word of the cross, as those who for themselves trust Jesus Christ as Savior and Lord.

An Urgent Call

With that, we are called to identify with the church's mission of being the Lord's agents in taking this word to the rest of mankind. If universalism were true, there would scarcely be a missionary task. There could scarcely be any urgency to tell people of the Savior whom they need. If they didn't hear in this life, they would hear in the life to come, and they will all be saved in the end anyway.

But according to the Bible, it's not like that. Believers who know the sovereignty of God working through the word to save sinners must recognize also the authority of the divine command to "go and tell," for this is the only hope of life for needy men. So we are left, as Christian people, with a task to perform. Mission is our usual name for it.

Strictly speaking, the Christian mission includes good works as well as evangelism, Samaritanship as well as church planting, social action as well as the proclamation of the gospel. But there is no question that evangelism must come first. I conceive it as a mistake when these two aspects of the Christian mission are made coordinates.

Surely the truth of the matter is that the purpose of the good works is to give credibility to the good words, and so by all means to further the message and induce men to believe it, to receive it, to trust the Christ whom it holds forth, and in him to find life. As in Jesus's own ministry, his works of love, healing, feeding the hungry, and so on, were meant to make credible and to confirm and establish his identity as Messiah and God's Savior, and so to draw men to trust him.

General Index

Scripture Index